DOUBLE TAKE

PORTRAITS OVER TIME

MAGGIE EVANS SILVERSTEIN

Books & Books Press

DEDICATED TO:

Bernie, of course.

My first two beautiful subjects, Jennifer and Joshua.

My twelve sparkling grandchildren: Julia, Lila, Sophie, Molly, Ava, Hannah, Asher, Benjamin, Ethan, Max, Jonah, and Will.

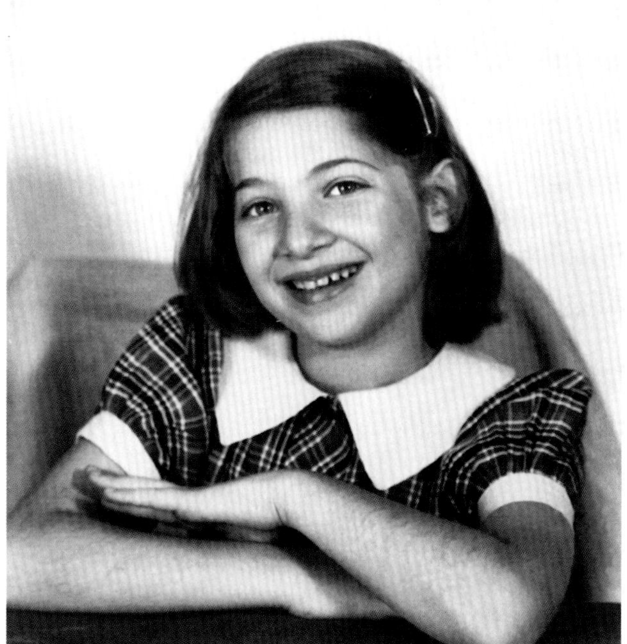

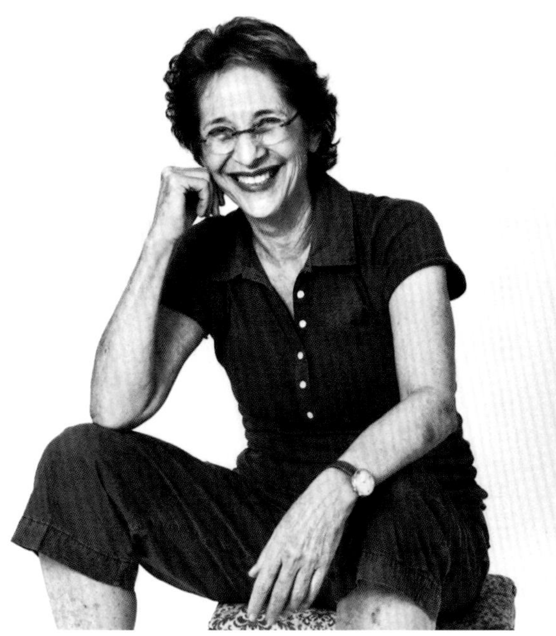

I AM TEN YEARS OLD
walking down the Raeford Road in short shorts.

I AM SIXTY-FIVE
I have twelve grandchildren.

On any given day if you should ever sit quietly and think very quickly through your own history, certain things would pop up, others would lay low. But what would always be true is how fast time goes.

DOUBLE TAKE

MAGGIE EVANS SILVERSTEIN

It's a March morning in Miami, one of those mornings when you already start to miss what we here call winter, those days when a fresh little breeze comes in with the cat. I'm in my studio, waiting for my client. I go out on my second-story porch that fronts South Miami's version of Main Street — I pull the blinds apart and look up and down the street. I go down my stairway and stand on the sidewalk looking this way and that. When a light sweat settles on me I go back upstairs and look at the kid's photographs from an earlier shoot — he's standing on a little chair in his diapers, he's draped over his mother's shoulder, weeping. How he wants to go home! Now I hear footfalls on the stairs and rush to the door just as the knock begins.

It's my client. He's smiling; he has a beard.

Almost twenty years have gone by since I set up shop as a black-and-white portrait photographer, and the young man I was about to photograph was someone who grew up in my sight. Now he was on the verge of leaving home and I knew how his mother would look at this new image, her good-bye boy. And if I got it right today, if when she looked into this earnest face and recognized him so thoroughly and maybe glanced back down her wall of photographs to that earlier time, she might experience that combustible feeling of joy and sadness, longing and relief. What we all feel when touched by the trajectory of our children's lives.

I love this job.

I began the work of taking photographs in this studio up this very stairway and my current clients are, for the most part, my old clients. When I began, they brought their babies to me: the mom might hold them close; the dad might turn them upside down; they would cry; they would giggle. And, in time, many of these children would come back, the solemn teenagers, the exuberant leaving-home kids, the wedded couple . . . the new babies. One client has put these years in small images, at eye level, all around one room. Time can, in a way, make you dizzy.

What you'll be looking at in these pages — or perhaps you already have if you, like me, look at pictures first and read the text later — are photographs of a child alone or with siblings or with parents and next to each is another image, taken after some time has gone by. And not any particular time; the second image may be after only a few years or much longer, to give notice to a birthday, a First Communion, a Bar Mitzvah. Leaving home. And once, just as parents were divorcing, as a future gift to the child, the last family picture.

These photographs side by side, these diptychs — and in some cases, triptychs — speak about the swiftness of time, how before we know it a childhood passes by in front of us. We can't, of course, see it in our daily lives — but aren't there times when a child may suddenly turn to look at you and there it is, you see the adult who will come? In these side-by-side images the children might as well be saying, watch what happens, I'm traveling between the frames, slipping into more of who I will be.

My studio in the little town of South Miami never changed much over the years. For twenty years, there were termites. We were tented and *still* had termites — Miami! And the concrete stairway always looked cruddy. Sometimes at night people sat and ate on the stairs and left their greasy things there. Sometimes people would pee there. (Mornings, I'd fill a bucket with hot water and throw it down the stairs.) But once inside . . . it was a great open space with high ceilings. I used one strobe, a soft box, and a second light sometimes but it fell over once and suffered a big dent on its metal hood, so after that, not so often.

It was a setup that intimidated no one.

Word of mouth brought people to me. When they would come to check me out I would say, "Years from now when you look at these photographs, I don't want you to say, 'How beautiful I look.' I want you to say, 'That's just the way I was.'" A lot of people would reply, "Well, I'll call you" — and never did. But to the ones who came back, I would say, "Don't worry about what you do in front of the camera; you can't do anything wrong." And so I would look at them, we would talk a little, a few hours would go by. Some people got irked by such a long process. Once, a two-year-old went to the door and said, "I leaving now." But almost always, afterward, there has been a commonality. I would look at the images on my contact sheets, far more than a more confident photographer would have taken, and it was so like reviewing interview notes I once took as a journalist, when I worked for *the Miami Herald*: You begin to see what is true. And what isn't.

In time, this lovely thing began to happen. I would look at a little girl; she's wearing a print dress her mother has made for her (little flowers), and she has brought her fluffy boa with her and wrapped it around her neck. In the photograph she stands facing me with a look that says she is already older than this. Later, much later, when she comes back, a little past her appointment time — sorry, she'd been looking for a parking space — she gives me just what I am looking for: that gorgeous, unwavering straight-on gaze. Could I see that old child in the new young woman, arm thrown over the back of her chair, still looking straight into the eye of the viewer? I start to pull out the fluffy-boa photos and put them next to ones I have just printed. And I begin to stack the diptychs.

So much of what happens in the studio has, of course, already been settled, long before the session: the bond (or not) between the subjects, and the one between them and me. I go to a client's house, sit on the bed while we look in the closet. Sometimes I might hear, "I don't like anything," but little by little we layer pants, shirts. We might think about bringing along a chair, maybe a pet. We're in agreement. In one house, as I'm ready to enter the third and youngest sibling's room, he locks his door. His mother begs him to open it and after about a half an hour, he does. In the shoot, we get along great. In one image, he's on his knees between his two older siblings and his arms have shot straight up into the air — victory!

I try not to plan too much ahead; I don't want to see myself reflected back. On the morning of a shoot, I'm always a little uneasy. What makes me think I can do this? I've promised what they'll wind up with is some recognition of themselves. What if this morning they're tired or sick or I can't think straight, or right, or at all. I'm soothed by looking at landscape photographs in William Eggleston's *The Democratic Forest*. They're so beautiful. In their veracity, I want my portraits to look like his pictures. One is a field with a big blue sky and clouds that cover 90 percent of the image and, then, a line of trees, on the verge of spring, just this sweet little row in the distance. But my favorite, which I have stared at for so many added-up hours, is of a white spitzy kind of dog, his head a little down, yawning, sitting beside a sidewalk and under a blooming dogwood tree. It's called *House Dog at Home*.

When my clients show up, if their children are little, I grab them right away, before they can balk. Or before they go to sleep. Otherwise, we hang up a change or two of clothes on the rod in the bathroom, maybe talk a few minutes. "If I ask you to do something," I say, "tell me if you don't want to."

I look at their bodies, how they fit with one another or with themselves, geometrically, emotionally. I try to keep things moving so their pause won't become a freeze, so they'll lapse into their own comfort instead. If I find I'm over-telling them what to do I also might say in a motherly voice, "I know, I'm bossy." I look through my camera at the edge of the frame, watch for the elbows, the hands, a foot. When I think I see just what I want to see, I say, "Stay there!" in a voice of such urgency that even I find weird.

What still seems a mystery to me is that staring over and over at portraits that are or are not my own has never stopped holding me in a beautiful grip. I look at the formal portraits from the 1850s, the nascent days of photography; I look at the crossed arms of the Depression-era farmer, of children playing by the hydrants on the streets of New York, of people who are invited to come in off the street into a studio in a small Midwestern town, of a little girl holding her dress out to each side in the dwindling light of her backyard. Each face is a curiosity. So much time has gone by. Did they become what they wanted? Were they happy? How did their lives turn out?

When I'm shooting and things aren't going well — someone's upset, doesn't want to be next to anyone, wants to leave — I can't give it up. I make promises I can't keep. Once a parent said to me on leaving, "This was the worst day of my life." Let me say, those pictures were great — full of velocity, energy. All that juice. Once in a while, someone is too passive, too willing, what do I want them to do — that's harder.

Sometimes the truth isn't pretty. A family is in front of me, two boys I shot years ago, frolicky, happy. Now one of the boys is mad, he's fifteen and he's been mad for three years. He doesn't want to be here, he doesn't want to be anywhere. I give him a chair, his mom cautiously goes to stand behind him. And now we smile over the boy's head, her arms wrap around his shoulders. The image is so strong: the dark son, the mother who loves him no matter what. Maybe, I think, in some other time he'll be standing beside her, quite a bit taller than she, arm around her, surveying the proof of her waiting for him.

My stack of "passages" grows. When I add a new one, I tend to thumb through all the others. What do they share, what do they answer? I search for why the meaning, which I can't quite identify, is so potent for me and why I am so struck with tenderness whenever I do this. That embraces even the child who, when I had called out his name one time too many as he was held in the arms of his horrified parents, spat at me. Childhood is messy. After a shoot, when a parent comes to look at the first small prints, she will often, as she picks up each one, talk about the child and tell me how he's getting along, what his feelings are, and how maybe this is what she's seeing in a photograph. And almost always there are other things I come to know about the years in between. When they are sad, they break your heart — the divorces, a dad who's gone to jail for mortgage fraud, the cancers, the honey-sweet only child who ends up in reform school. The young mother, jogging on the side of the road, run over. And when they are good, that lives in your heart, too — the little ones beaming along, the beautiful new grown-ups filled with their loves and their work. I feel like a first-grade teacher — they are, somehow, my children, too. Because they let me look at them, over time. They know my longing, because I tell them: "Think about time passing and what it will be like to turn around and recognize yourself, just as you are now."

I photograph a young man with his siblings and alone. He's thirteen. I print the image of him alone but it's not one his parents choose: he's wearing a too-big thrift-store army jacket, he's so unhappy. Years later he comes back, a beautiful young man with his siblings; they're a dream to photograph. A few more years go by; I get an announcement of his wedding. As a gift, I send the adolescent photograph. I get a letter back:

"Thank you for the gift of your picture of me in the army jacket. It arrived with my parents the morning after our son Homer was born and I looked at that picture of me and thought, for the first time, I remember him. And I am still him, of course, but it was helpful to me to see where I was and how much heaviness I carried with me. I have grown into myself and can better carry that weight, whatever it is. My wife loves the picture too — the boy she would one day marry."

When the time came for me to close the studio and to close this project, I asked the almost or mostly grown-ups or, sometimes their parents, to look at these images, side by side, and tell me what they saw. And now you will see that is what they did, graciously and openly.

JUSTINE & NICHOLAS

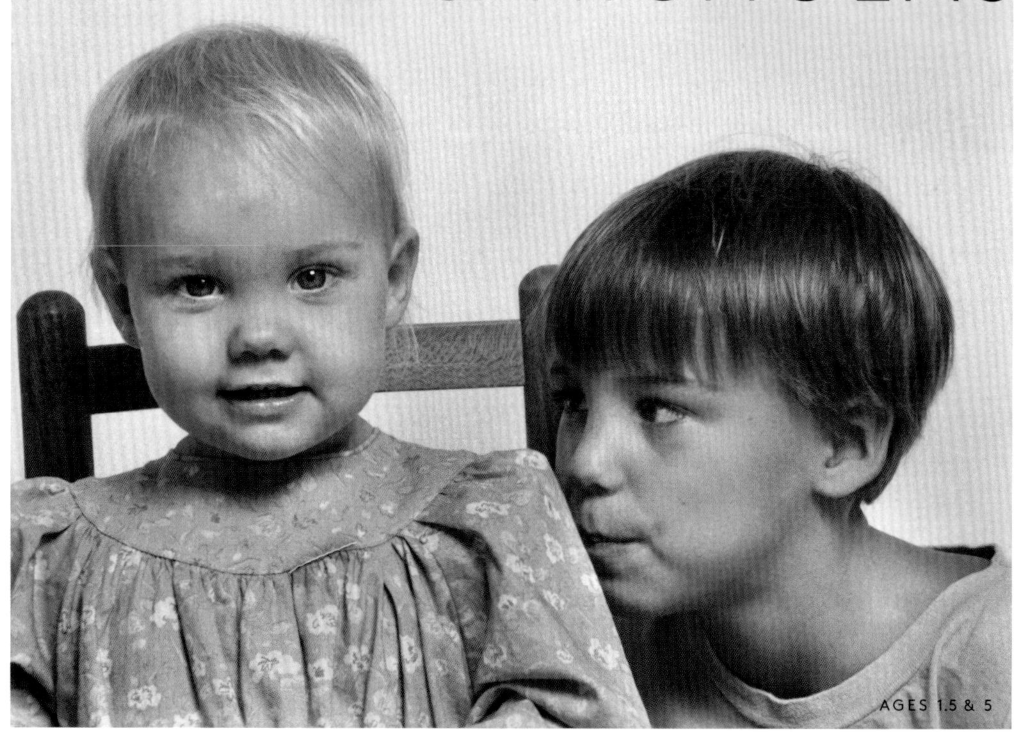
AGES 1.5 & 5

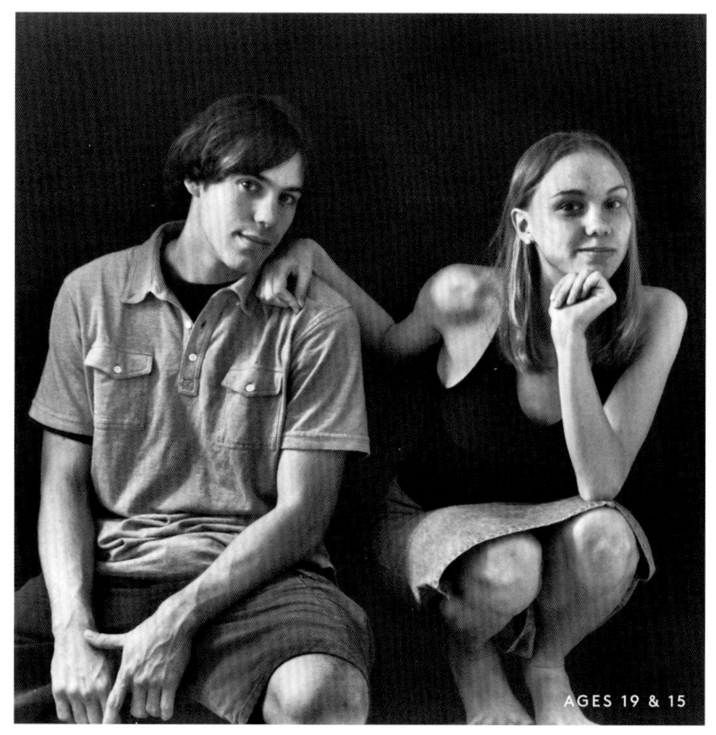
AGES 19 & 15

FOREWORD:

MADELEINE BLAIS, PULITZER PRIZE WINNER

When our daughter Justine was four or five years old, she had a friend whose parents tried to explain evolution to her. They were both Ivy League professors so lofty discussions came naturally to them. The child listened carefully and finally said she thought she understood: "Oh. We weren't us when we were going to be us." A parent's job with children is evolutionary in nature. It is to preside over a human version of photosynthesis in which, eventually with enough light and water and oxygen, we get them to be THEM. This concept of coming into your own self-identity is something children appear to understand intuitively, at least judging from an essay that Justine once wrote about our local famous poet: "Emily Dickinson is probably the most mysterious and shy of all poets. She always ran upstairs whenever the doorbell rang. She tried not to meet strangers. Although as shy as can be, the poems are the real her." I can't say when the blur began, but there comes a time when you stop documenting every milestone, first tooth, first smile, first step, and you sit back and let the process take care of itself. Days meld into one and another, and it's all a mush: ...the car pool machinations, the African dance recitals...the constant demand for new cleats, driver's school, driver's tests, and the number two pencils for the SATs. The time between then and now, between the first squawling greeting and the turning of the tassel from one side to the other at graduation does go by in a blink of an eye. It is over before you know it. One evening, not long ago while our son Nicholas and I were in the car, heading to his friend's house, the music on the car radio started to fade out just as we reached our destination. "It is always great," he said, "when the song ends just as you pull into where you're going." With children the song never ends and you never really know for certain where you are going,

ERIKA

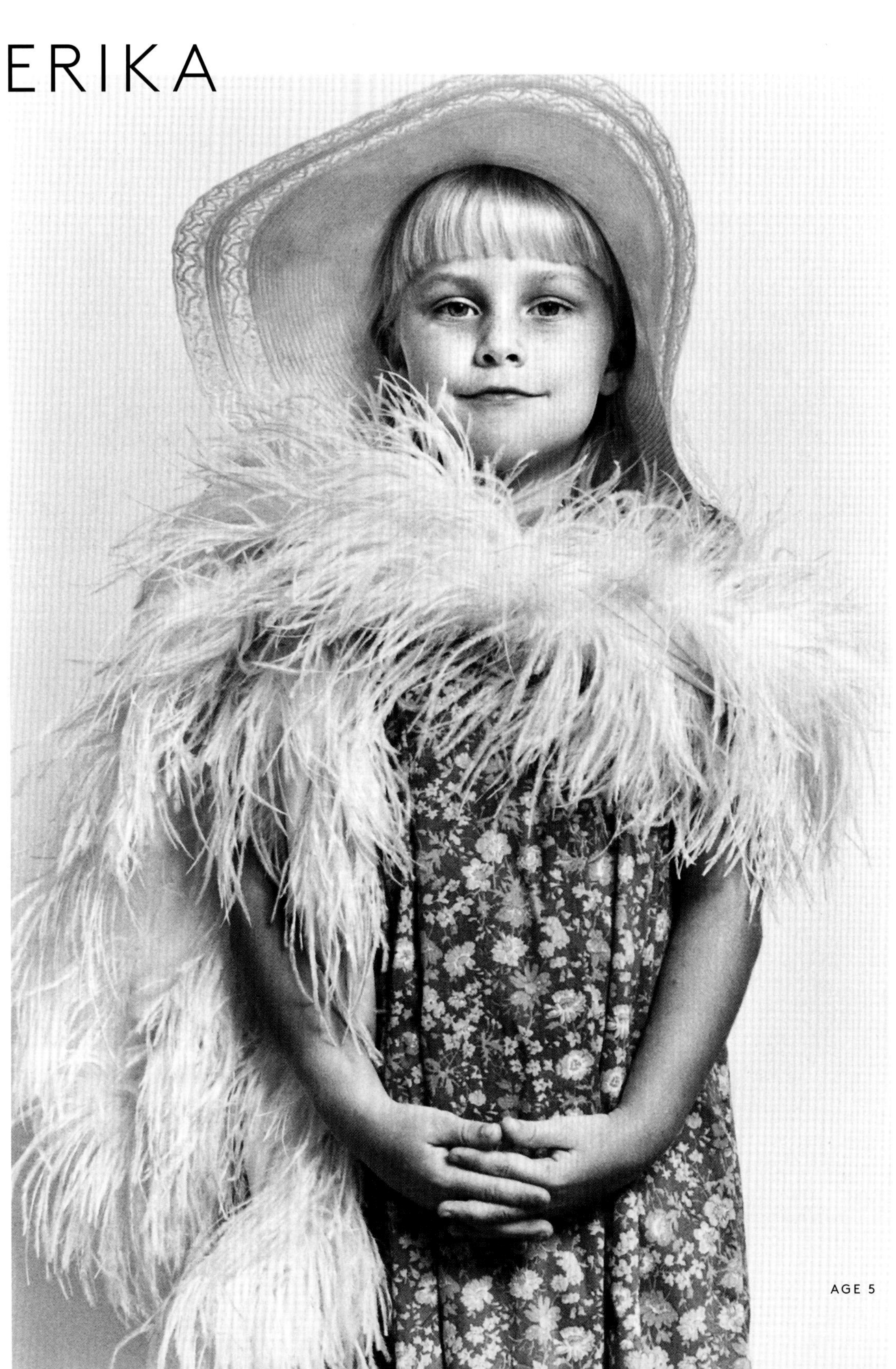

AGE 5

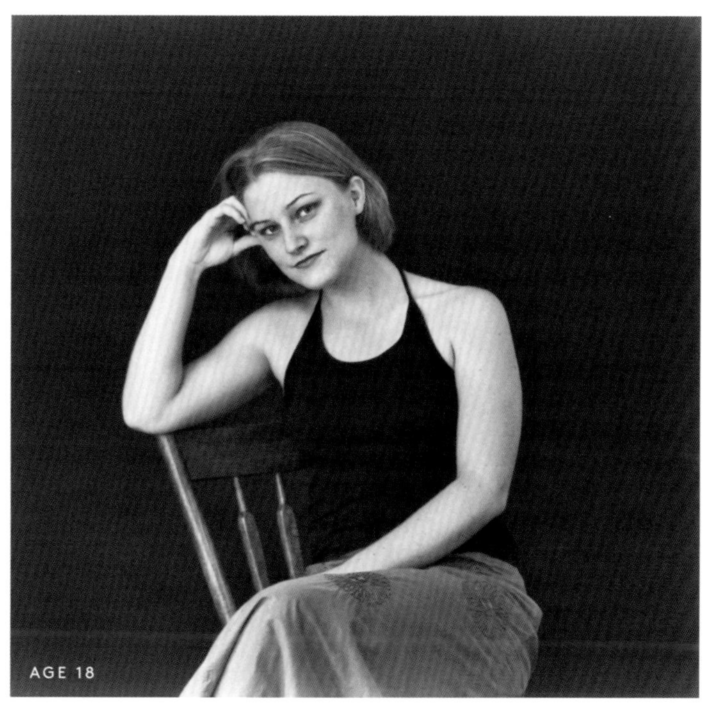
AGE 18

ERIKA, AT 29: Fantasy was a big part of my life, imaginary games. I'd be the mother or the teacher. I would convince my sisters that when we put on these dress-up clothes, that's who we were. My younger sister had the spotlight. I have always been more solitary. I was happy reading the same book five times in a row, not realizing that other people didn't do that. And even then, I knew that I wanted to be an artist. I became vulnerable. I had had serious back surgery when I was fifteen, the age when you want to fit in; I didn't want to feel fragile. Being around my mother was so important — she's very wonderful. Now, I don't have to second-guess myself. I can make my work more personal. I'm optimistic. These two people aren't the same. I'm much more aspiring to be my five-year-old self.

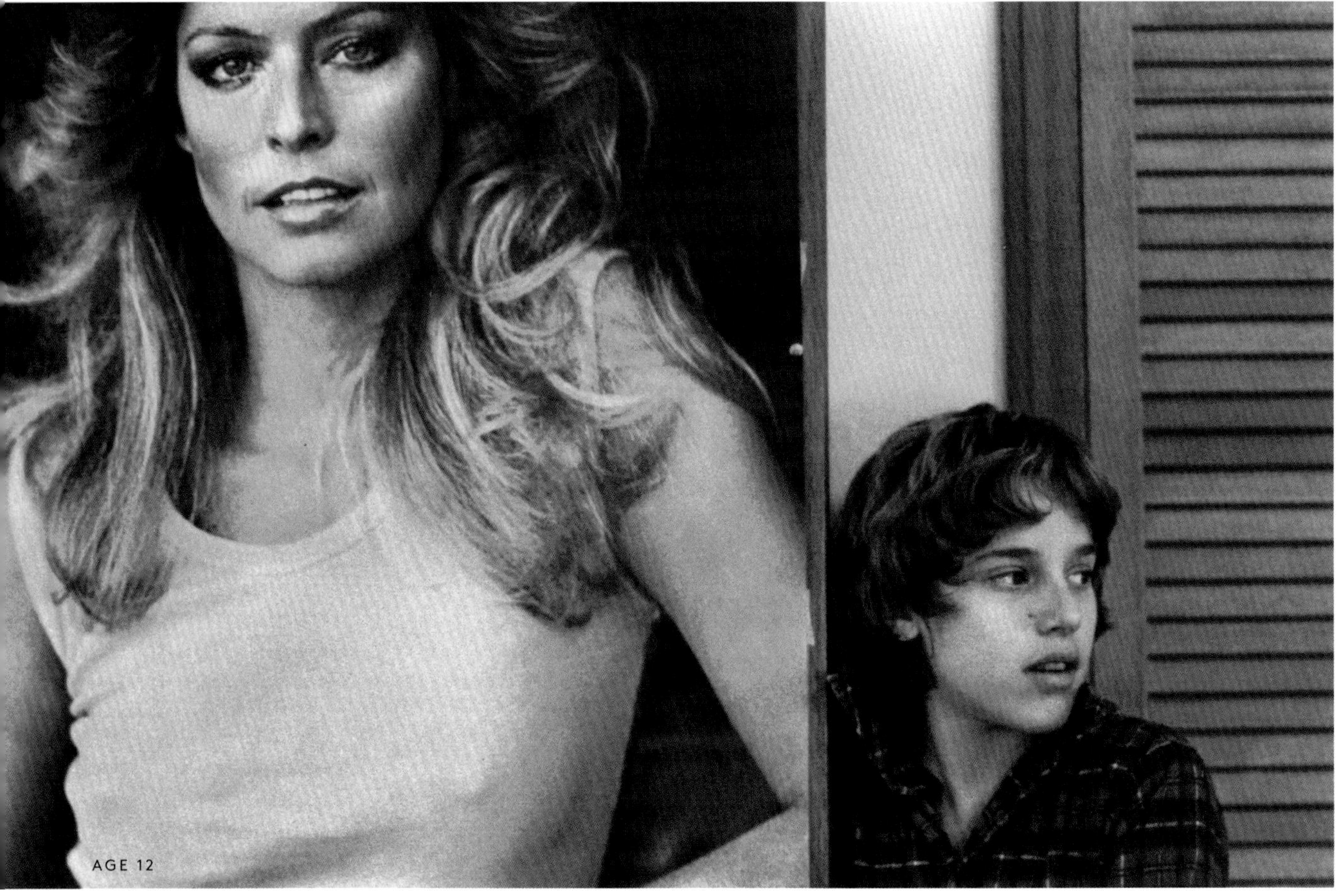

AGE 12

JOSHUA, THE SON OF THE PHOTOGRAPHER, AT 46: I chose that poster — it covered my entire door — because she was beautiful and strong. I'm looking away from Farrah so maybe I wasn't that comfortable. Also, I didn't like being stopped. I wanted perpetual motion. So I may be looking at something I wanted to do; I wanted to be over there. I would never recognize that person as me, physically. Maybe what I do recognize is the dual feelings of separate but connected that I still feel today. When I was twelve, my life was simple, uncomplicated. I was fun loving, impulsive. I felt carefree, roaming around the neighborhood with friends. I just thought about the present. I didn't worry. My parents allowed me to run around, rampant. I wanted that; I also wanted more advice, more check-ins. I still feel playful. There a switch in me that can go on and I can feel that age. My angst came later, when I was fourteen or fifteen. If you look at the picture of Ava and me sideways, it would look like we're lying down, just hanging out. I love my baby. I'm holding her tightly. I won't let anything bad happen to her. I'm kissing her. She trusts me.

JOSHUA & AVA

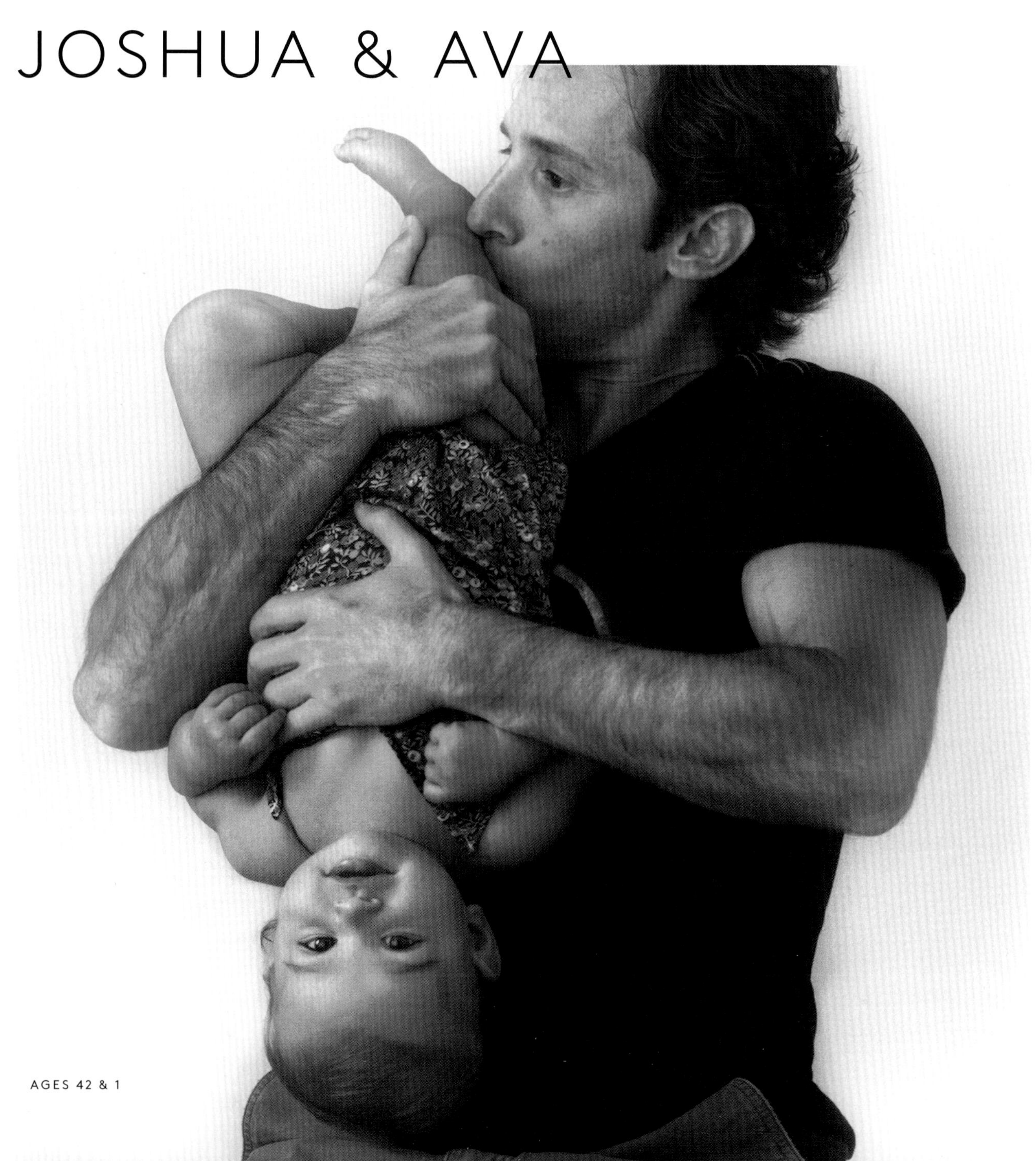

AGES 42 & 1

WILL & JULIA

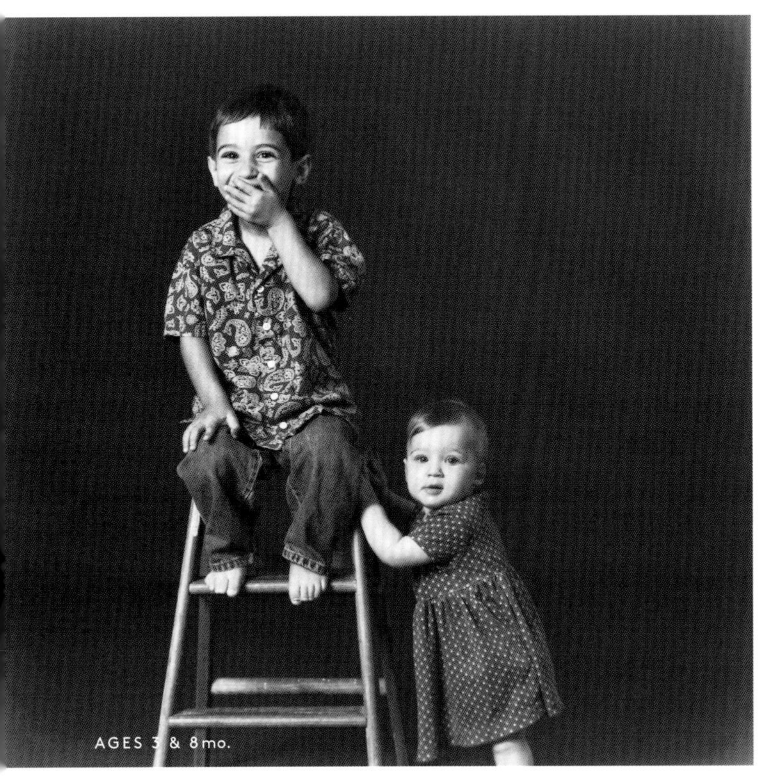
AGES 3 & 8 mo.

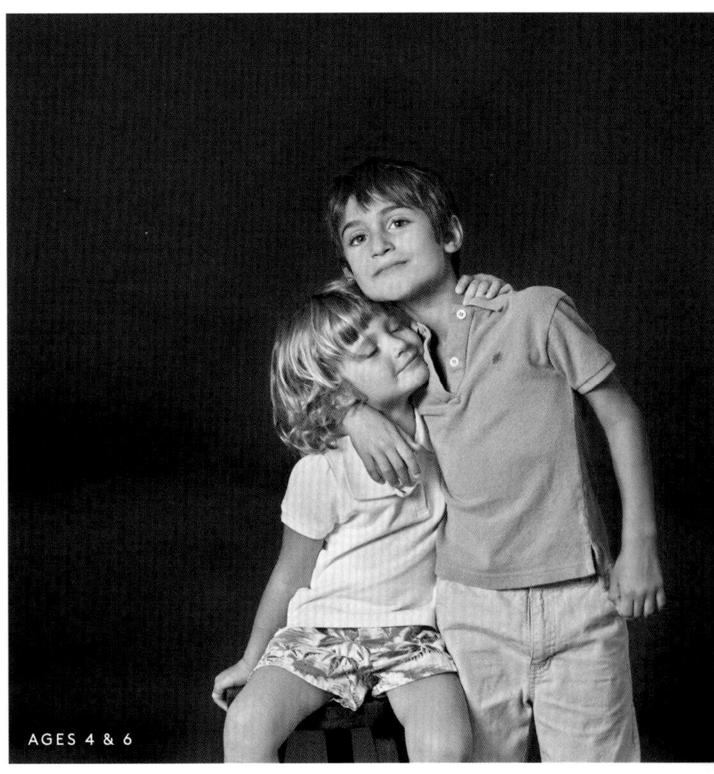
AGES 4 & 6

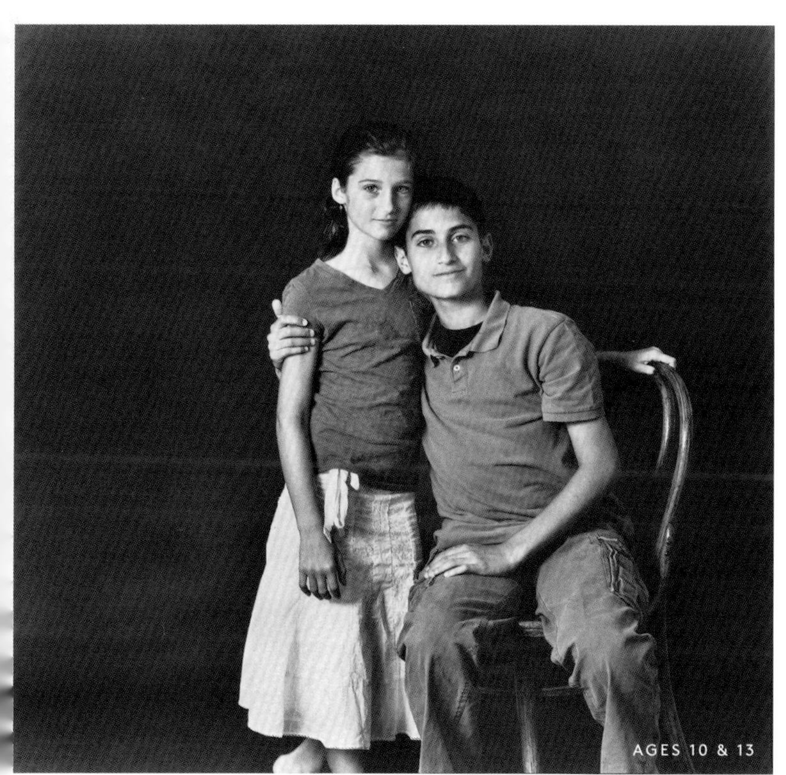

AGES 10 & 13

BOTH THE GRANDMOTHER AND THE PHOTOGRAPHER: In my house, I am being called from the small room with bunk beds that we call The Nursery: "Mamoooo, Mamoooo." My four-year-old grandson, who I had recently photographed with his little sister, isn't ready for sleep; the dusky light is seeping in through the window blinds. "Where," he wants to know, "did I come from?" "From Mommy's tummy," I say, with assurance. "No, no, no," he says reaching out for my hand. "Where was I before that?" Now, six years later, we're looking at the first two photographs, which are already in the past; he's ten. "That was an interesting question," he says, "but not one I think about now." I go on, revisiting for him how he once shared the wonders of his little mind, probing, probing, probing him until he gently announces, "Interview over," and as he pushes away from my dining room table says, "This was one of the most uncomfortable experiences of my life."

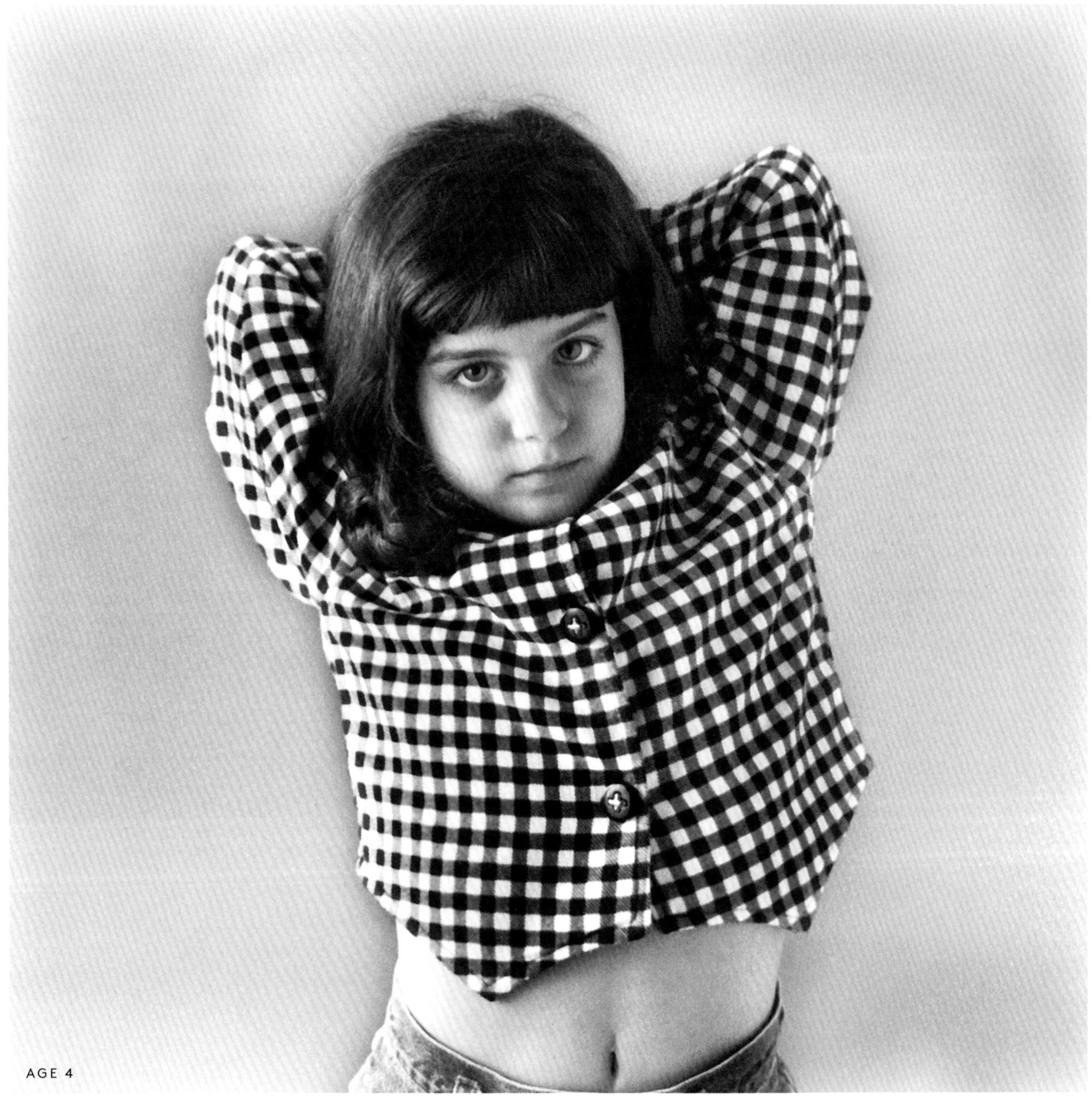

AGE 4

ABIGAIL, AT 24: The second picture is my senior yearbook picture. I look like such an adult. I wanted to look like that. I've always been tough, determined, decisive. Still, it's more adult than I feel now. My mom used to read me the *Runaway Bunny*. She bought the poster for my room. "You know," she said, "wherever you go, I will follow you." I think I'm pretty predictable. There's nothing crazy in my life. The day I told my parents I wasn't going to law school was the wildest I got. I love my work now. I recently had to pack up my room where I had grown up. I'm not sentimental. What I took with me was a photograph of my brother and me. I think about your other portraits. So many of us started from the same place. But things happen in the white space in between and afterwards. Parents divorce or die or go to jail. There are catastrophes that change lives. We've moved out of our big house; my mom is in a little condo. On Saturday nights my boyfriend and I go out with my mom and my brother.

ABIGAIL

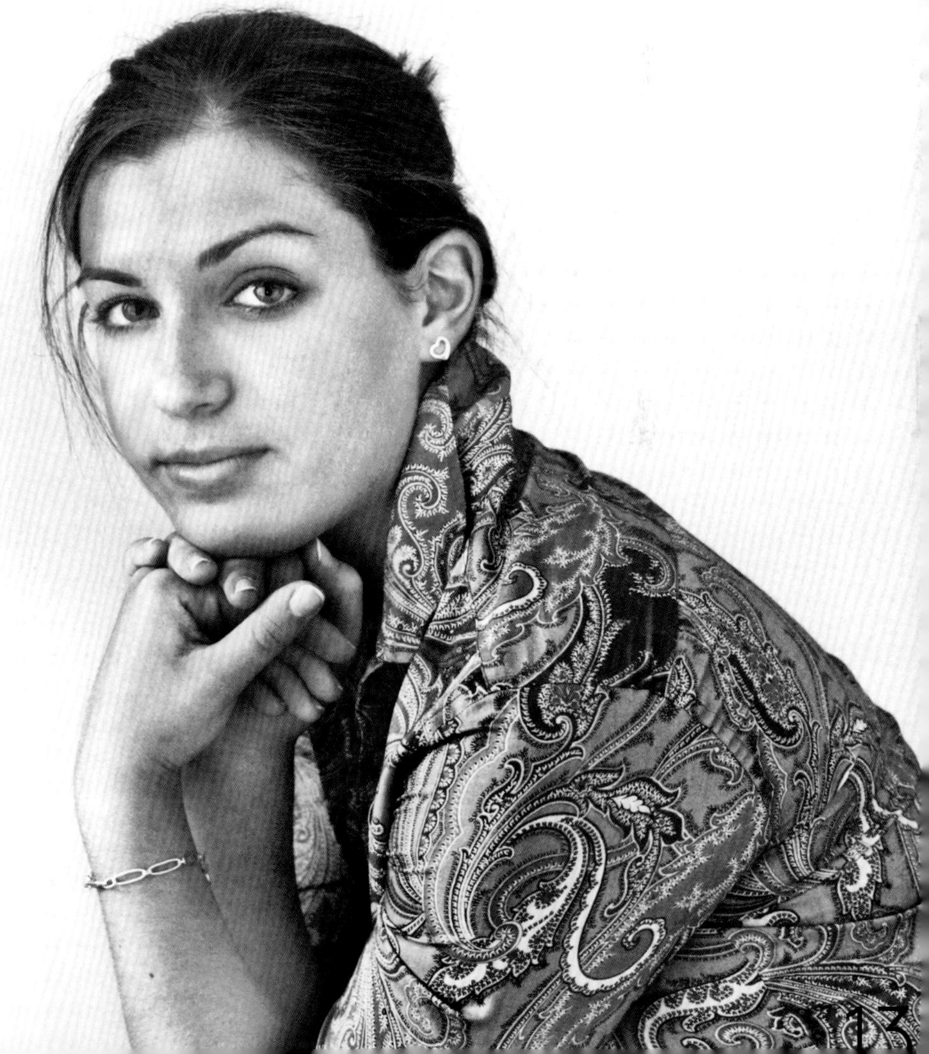

AGE 17

ALEXANDER, MARISA, NICHOLAS, RAYMOND, HAROLD & GABRIEL

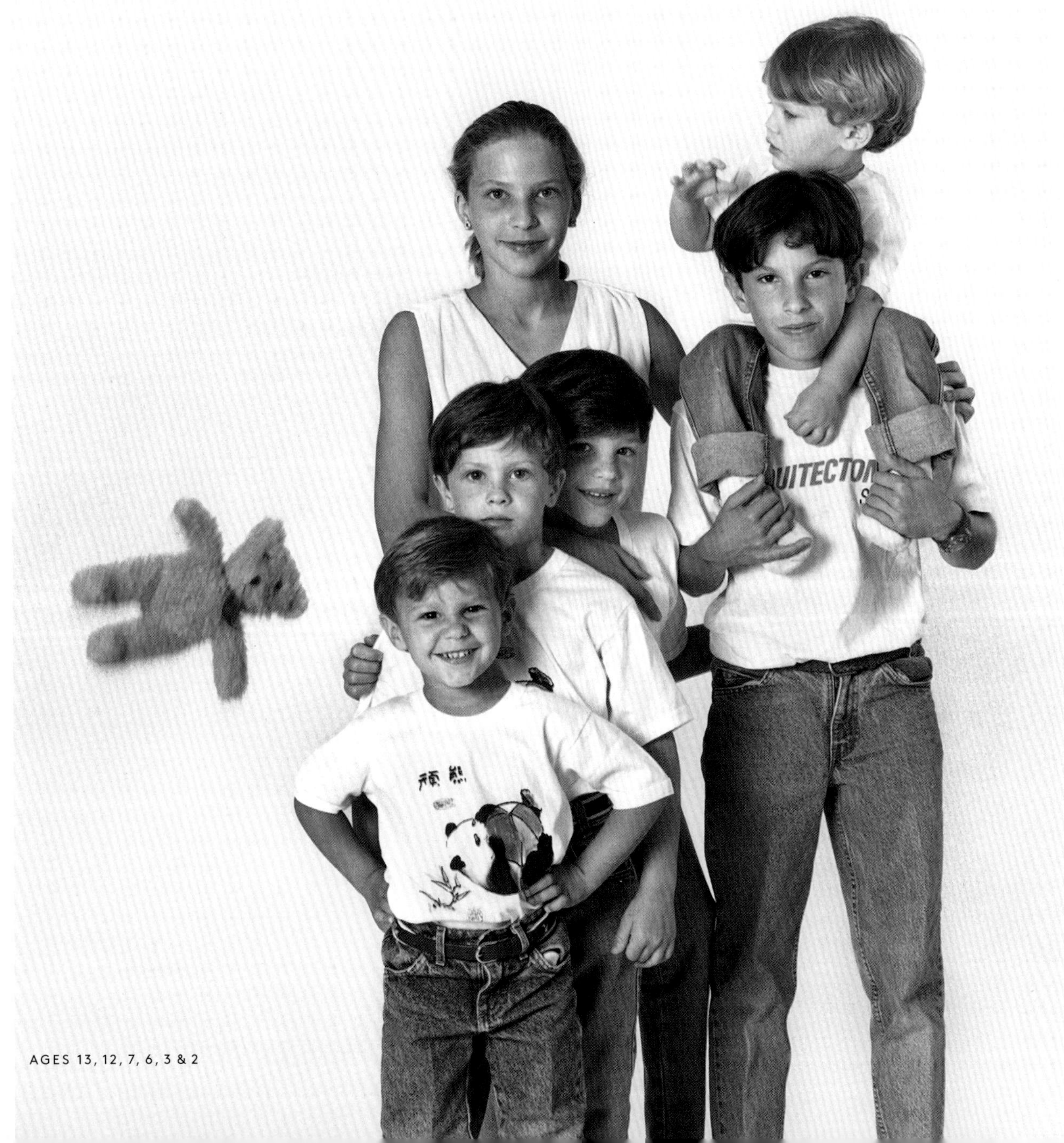

AGES 13, 12, 7, 6, 3 & 2

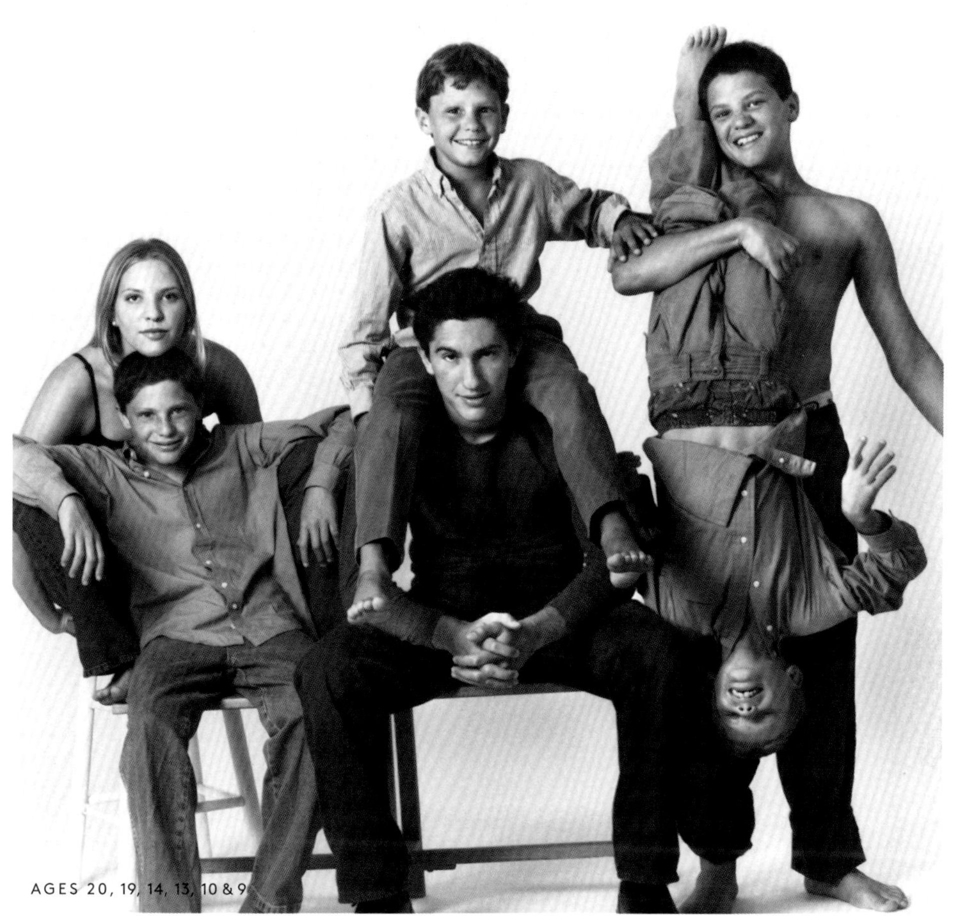
AGES 20, 19, 14, 13, 10 & 9

THEIR MOTHER: When my children were growing up, it was a halcyon time. There was no WWII of my parent's era, no Vietnam. We were living in a small town, Miami, that was becoming a big town just as diversity was beginning. The bay was their fun. They never went to a mall or watched TV. I never had to fight the battle of drugs and drinking; my parents were social drinkers but I never was. I think being an example means more than what you say. With my children no one feels more a favorite than any other.

LOUIS

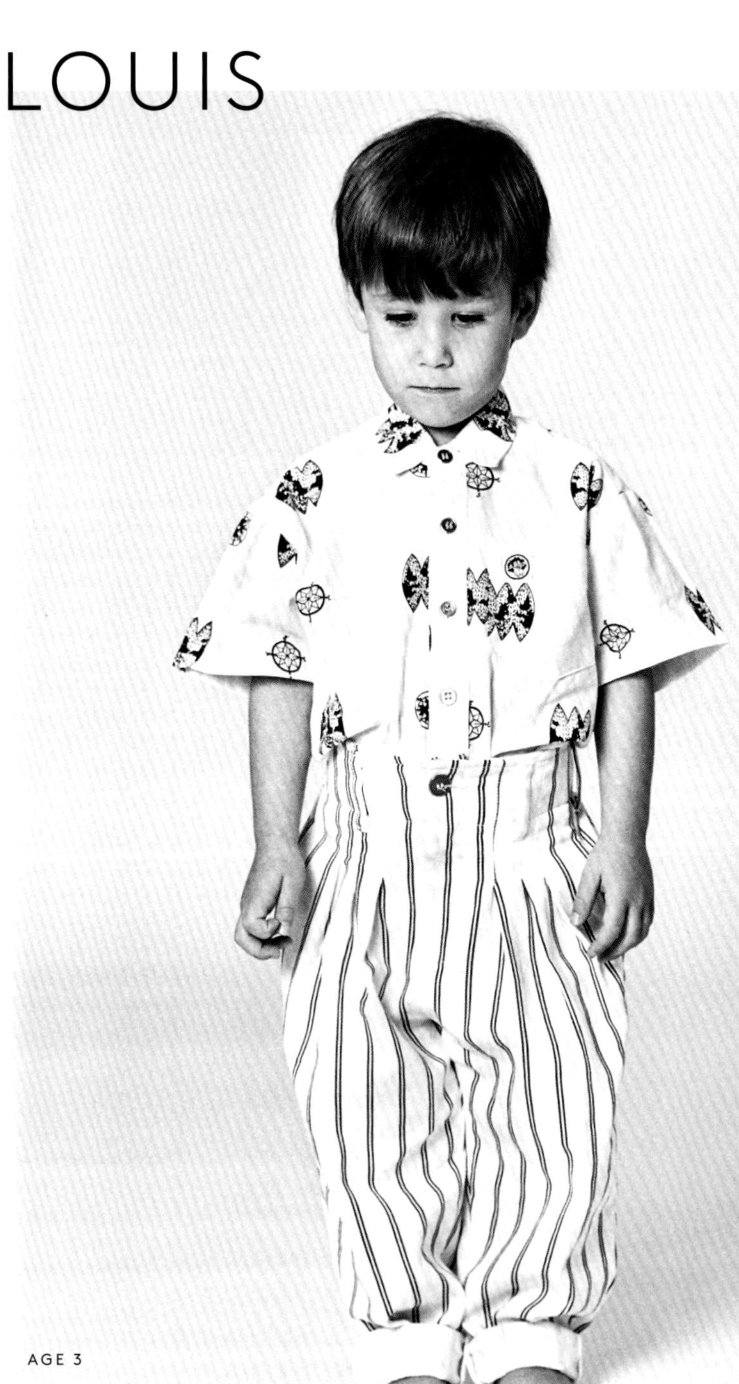

AGE 3

HIS MOTHER: He's my third. I was less intrusive with him than with the others. I see in this first picture an unambivalent sense of right or wrong. And in the second: as the world turns, you get flipped and flopped — "Ooph, I landed safely."

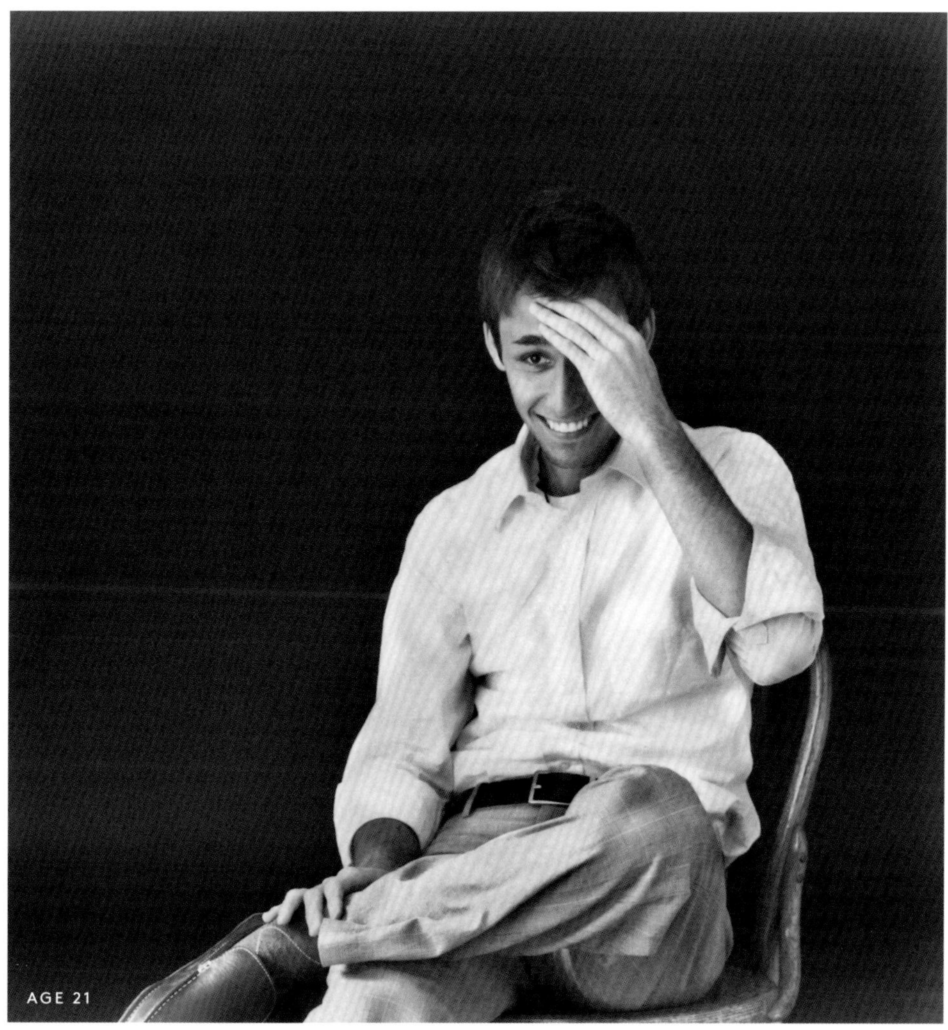

AGE 21

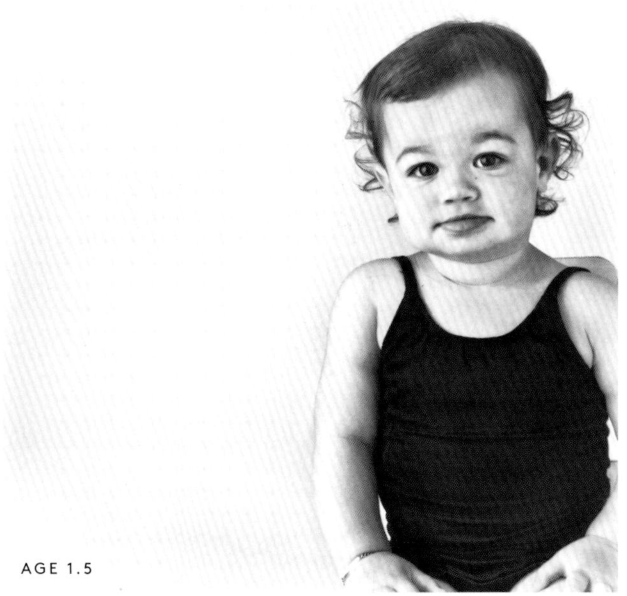
AGE 1.5

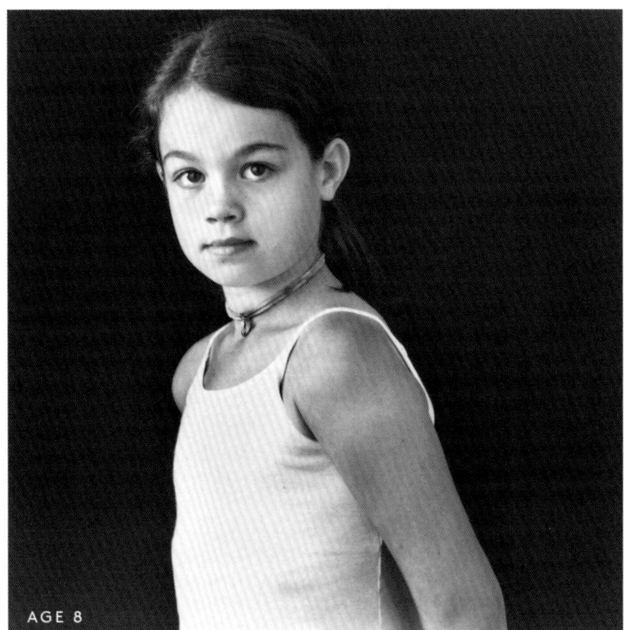
AGE 8

LILA, AT 10: I look more into the future than the past. I'm excited about that: what college I'll go to, what I'll look like. I picture myself with a job, being a chef or an artist. I don't think about having children. I don't know if I'll want them because I don't know what will be going on in my life. My parents know ninety-five percent about me. They don't really know my social life. I think life goes by slowly. I'm glad. When I'm doing something I love, it goes by fast. If I'm doing something I don't like, I know it'll be over.

LILA

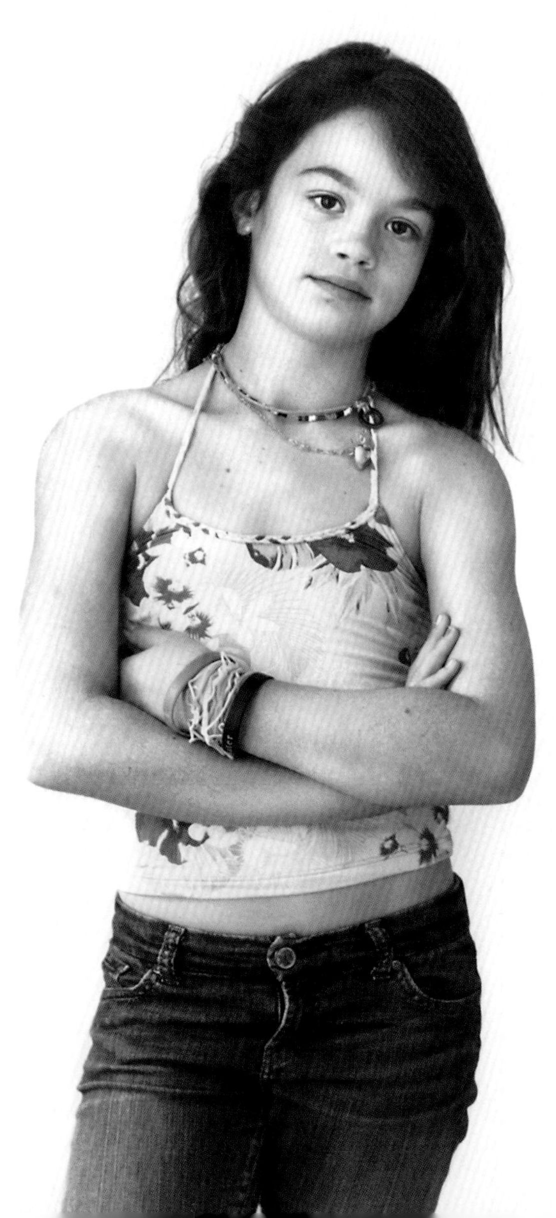

AGE 10

PETER & LILA

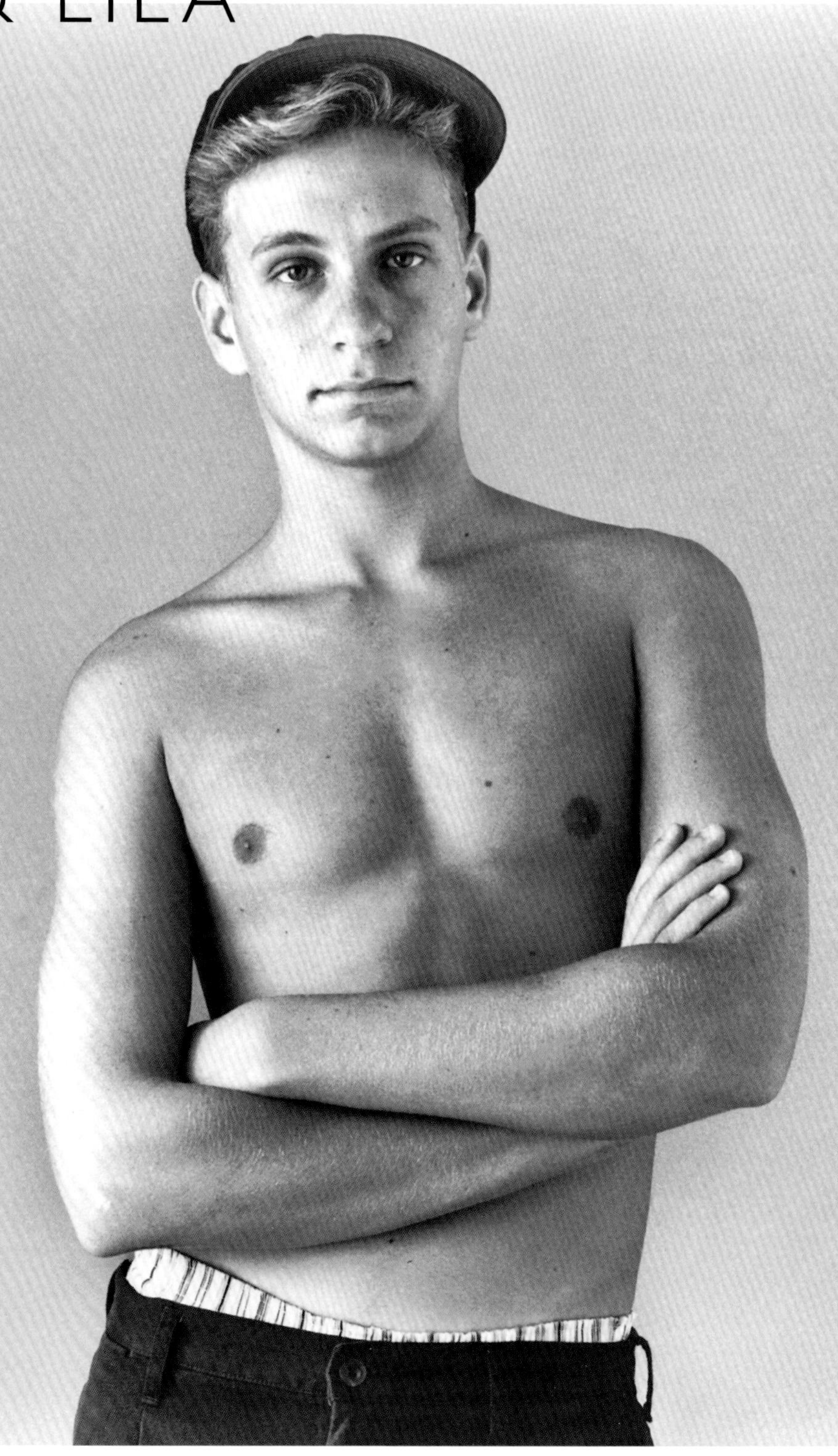

AGE 18

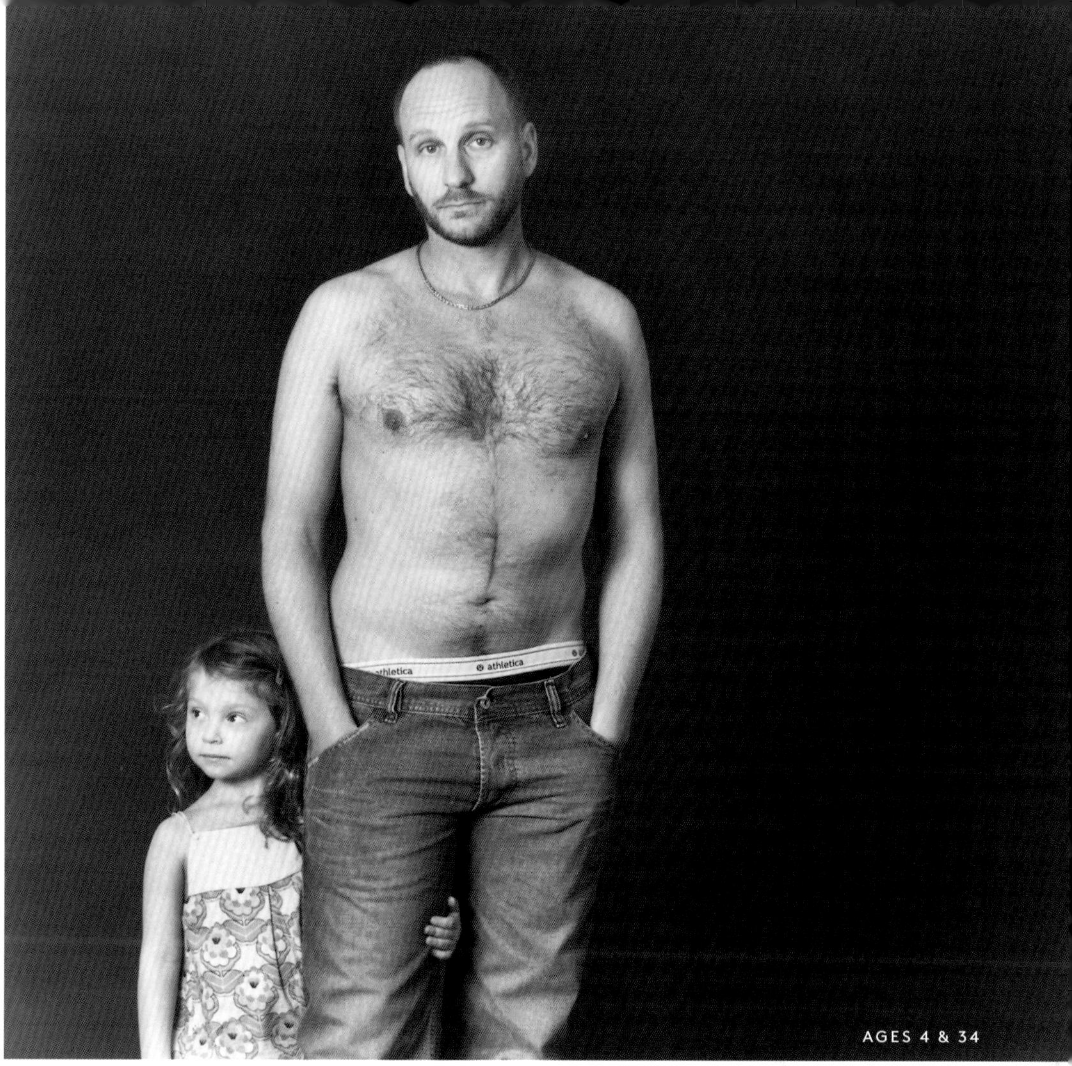

PETER, AT 36: I don't see too much of a difference between these two photographs. I used to go to school; now I go to an office. I don't see my childhood as over. I grew up in Miami and most of the kids I was friends with growing up, I'm still friends with. The same stupid conversations I had then, I have now. I knew my wife at thirteen — we have pictures of her at my Bar Mitzvah.

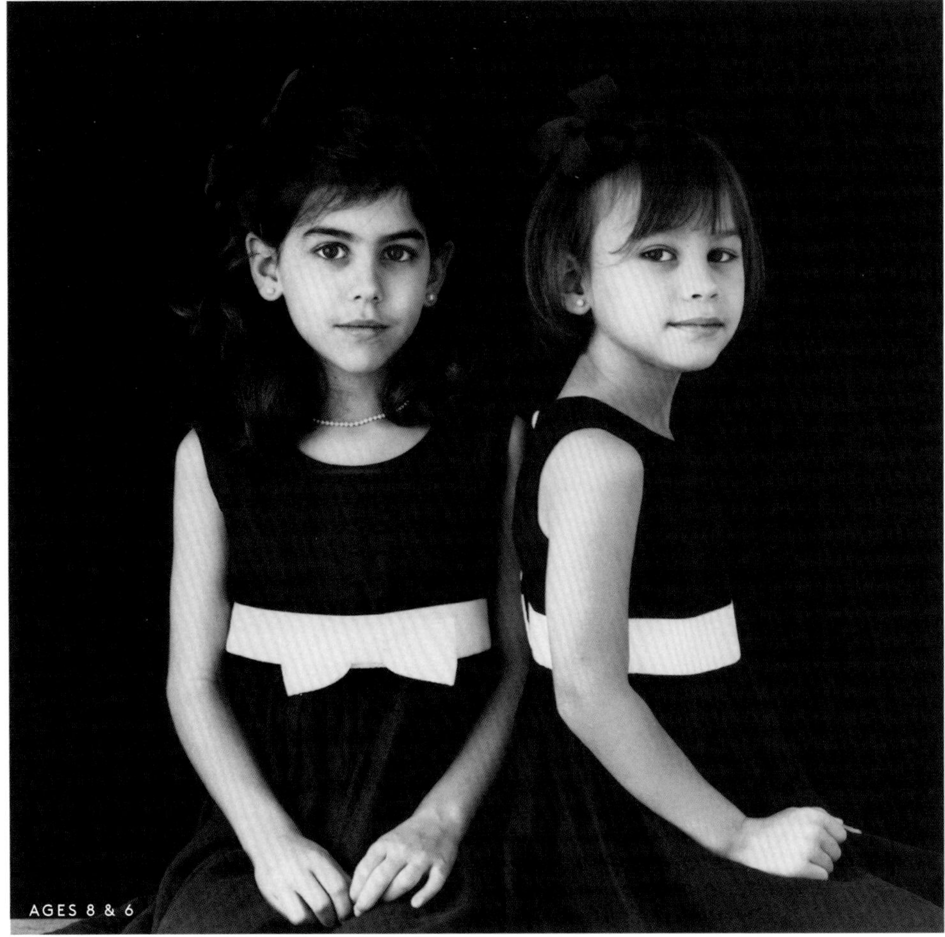

DANIELLE, ON THE LEFT, AT 22: You can see I'm reserved, careful, holding my hands on my lap. But look at my sister; she has a little bit of attitude, is more impulsive. You can tell we're blatantly different. I'm two and a half years older but she sees me as the little sister; she takes care of me. She looks straight at the camera; she's in charge, powerful. I don't have plans for the future. But I don't worry about it. I know there are always things to look forward to. Notice my sister in the second picture: she's being observed but she's also looking back at you; she's having a conversation with the viewer — "You figure it out, what am I thinking?" I'm an observer.

DANIELLE & VICTORIA

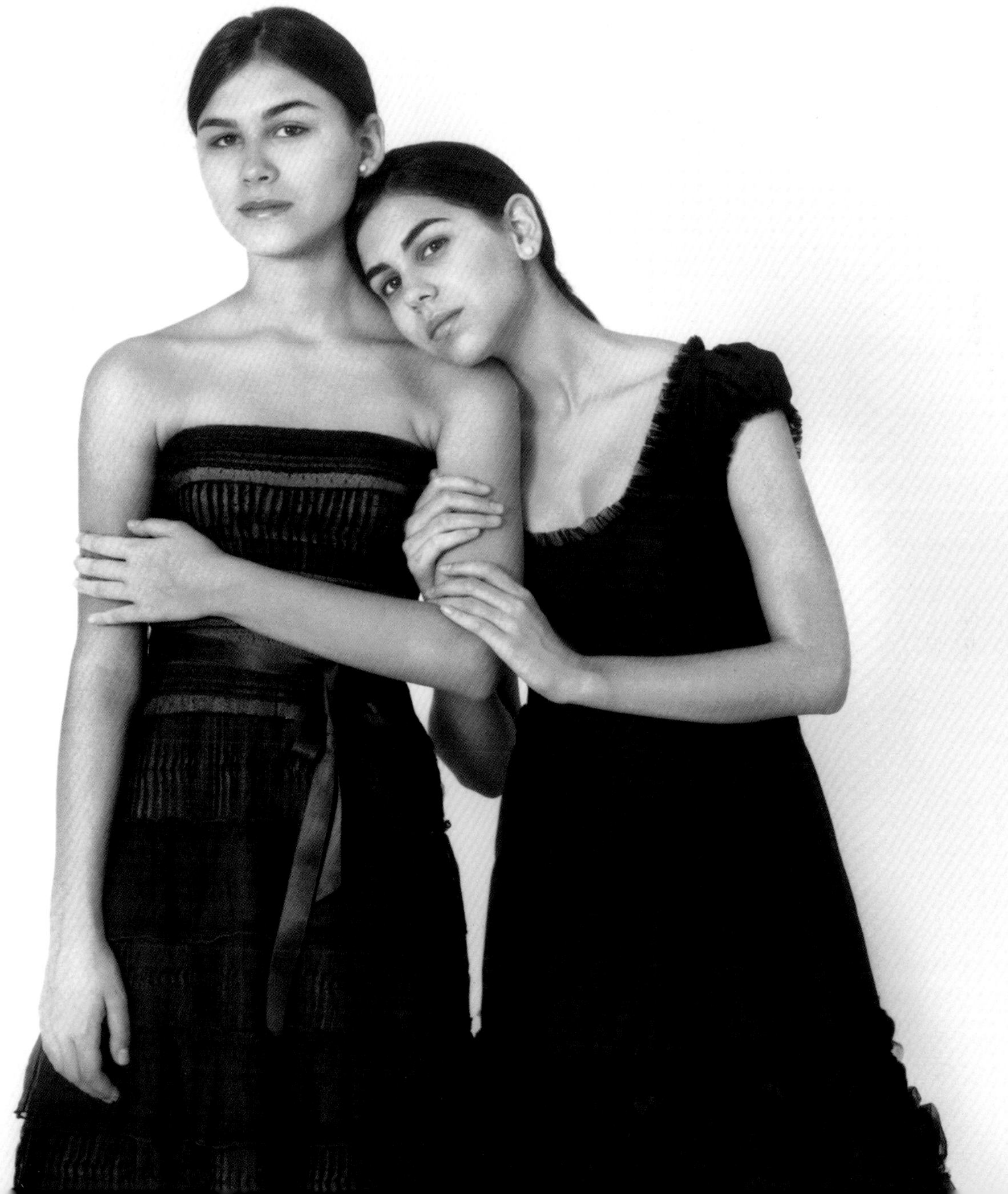

AGES 15 & 16

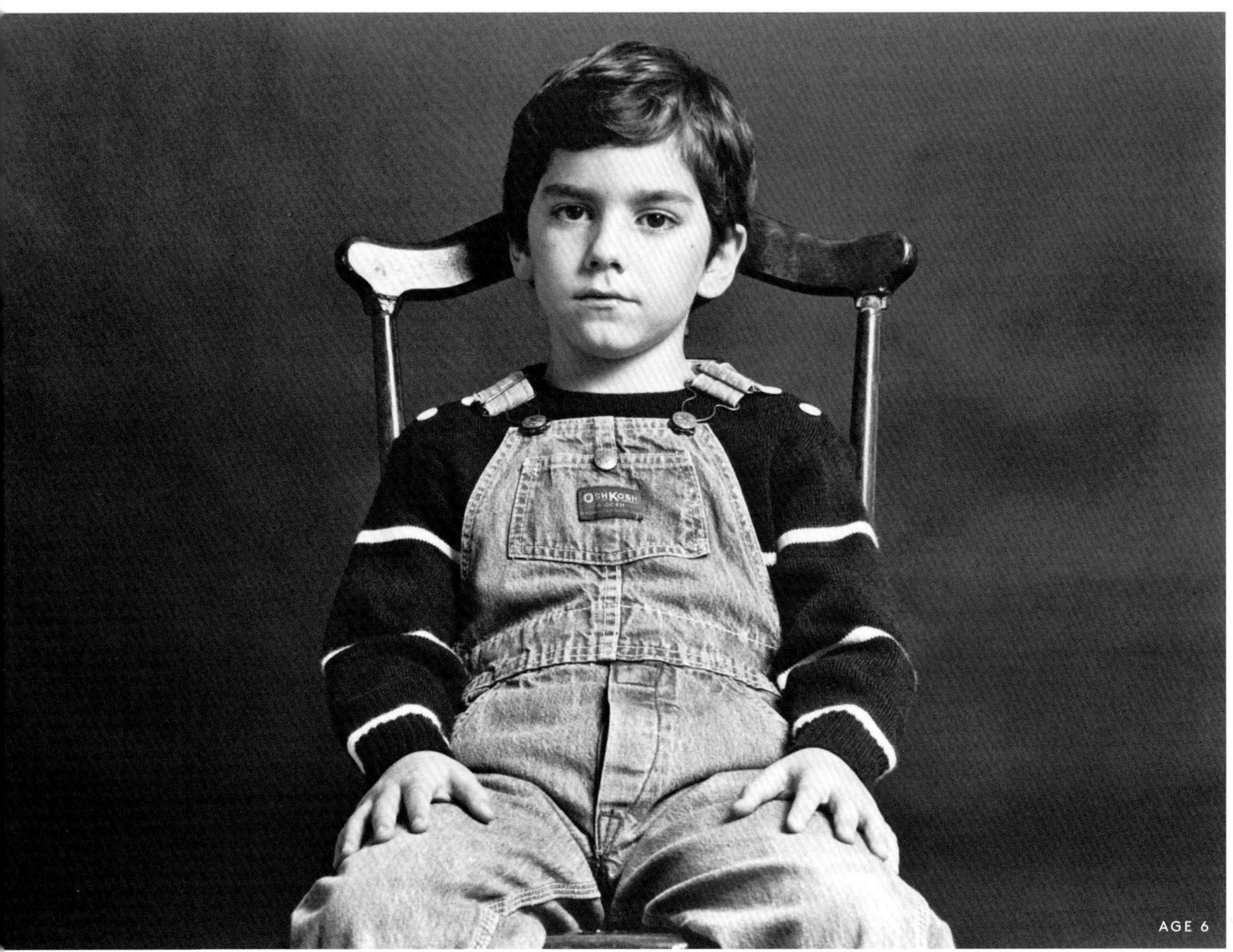

AGE 6

AT 29: When I was young, I'd look in the mirror and think about what I would look like later. When I looked at grown-ups, I thought about the divide — how would I change? I loved to draw. I had a paradise idea in my head. I'd be sitting on a patio. It would be raining but I wouldn't get wet. I would have my sketch pad and would be enjoying getting ready to draw something. I copied photos that I liked, drawing what I saw. I'm still committed to that same pursuit I had when I was drawing. But that transformed into playing the piano. Around sixteen, I had a shift. I'd hear a recording and I'd say, "I want to play that." I teach children and I can teach better when I catch a glimpse of myself as a little kid. I've sacrificed a little in the traditional trajectory of career. It has caused me some anguish when I don't believe in myself as a musician. When you look at these pictures together, they make a comment about mortality. Do they know? When you have the luxury of looking at the pictures, it makes that question very clear. Do they live with that director, that compass? The younger you are, the more engaged you are. You have more of a chance of seeing something new, of being mystified. What's old? Acquiescing to boredom.

HIS MOTHER: On his first day home from college he was playing basketball and broke his nose. He never fixed it. He said he was good with the imperfection.

ADAM

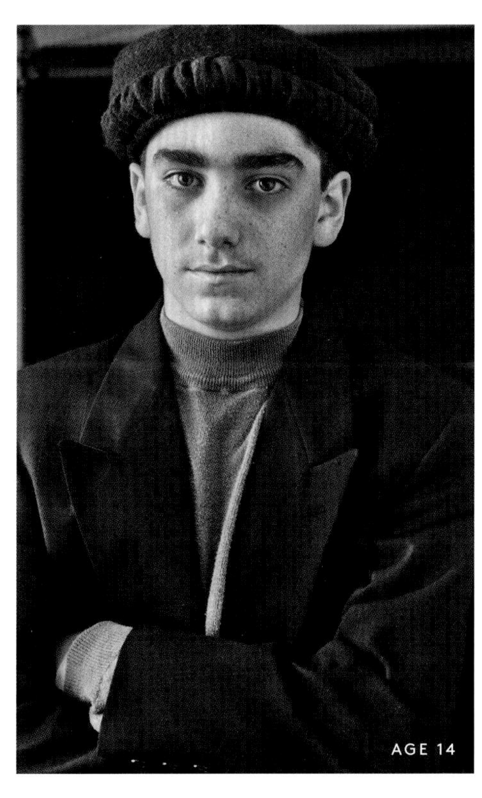
AGE 14

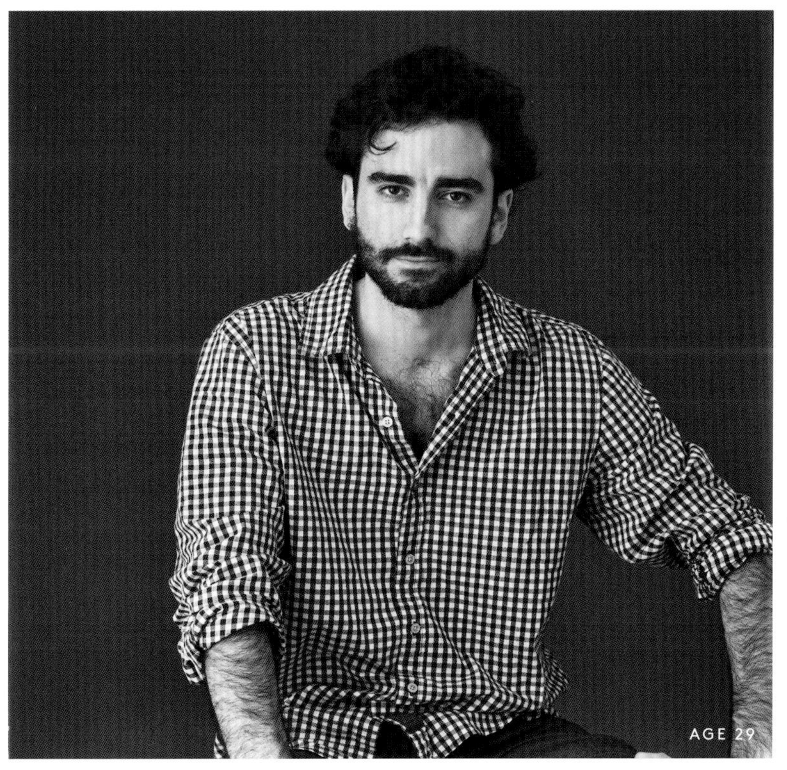
AGE 29

JONATHAN, NICOLE & NOEL

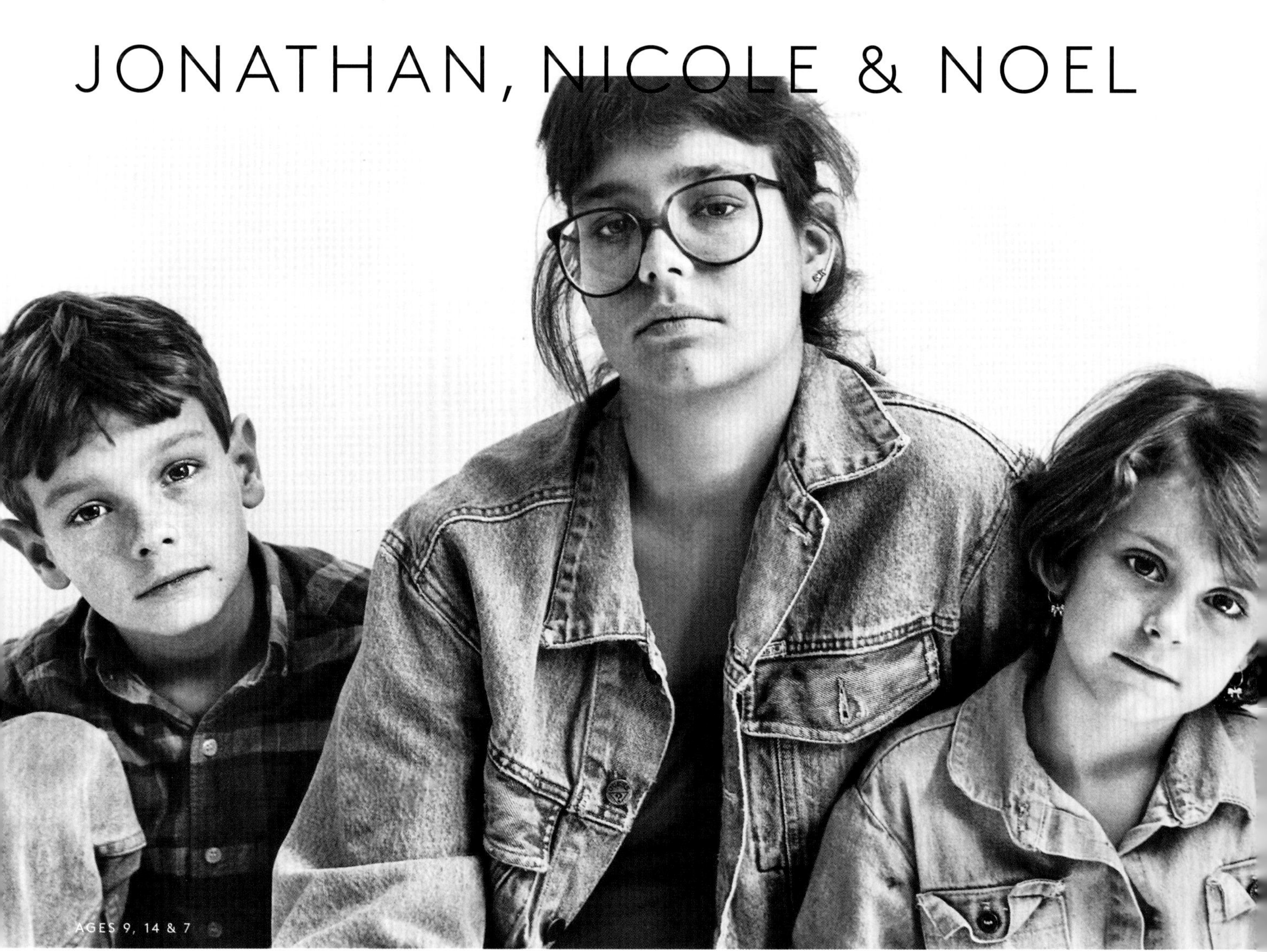

AGES 9, 14 & 7

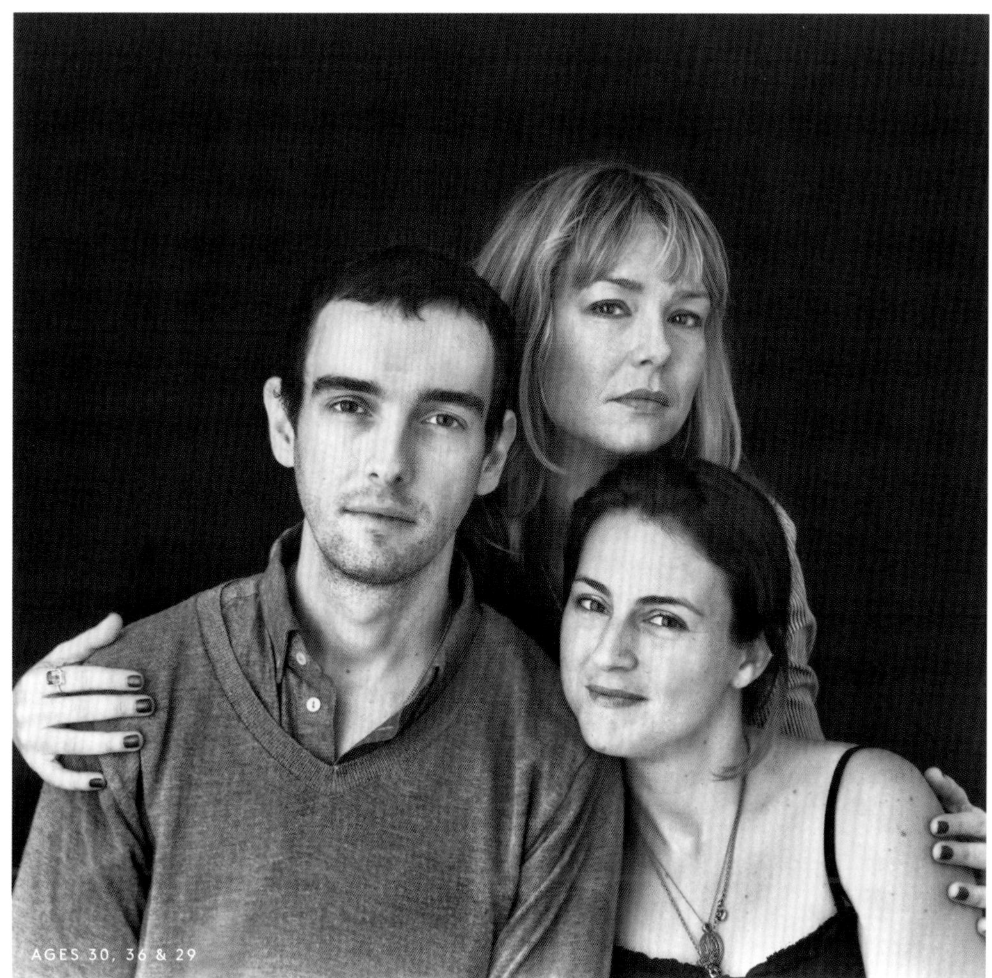

THEIR MOTHER: In the first picture, the children would not look at each other; they would not touch each other. They hated each other. And, look, here with the passing of time they haven't killed each other. Now I can look in their faces and see that they care about each other, they support each other. I had a hell-raiser. She was rebellious; I thought she might end up in jail. And now: she's the most loving, caring person who says she always wants to be in the same city with us. And I thought she would be the one to leave. At that age, they can't tell their parents that they suffer. You see, later, that you were so unaware of that. My son just bought a house—it's on a hill and a high school is close by. I was surprised when he told me he was going to get a big dog. He said the reason is that there's nothing more dangerous than a bored high school boy. You know you try to stay on top of things but you miss so much. My son told me, "I love how hard you tried, but we outsmart you at that age." I have a completely different relationship with them now: we're friends.

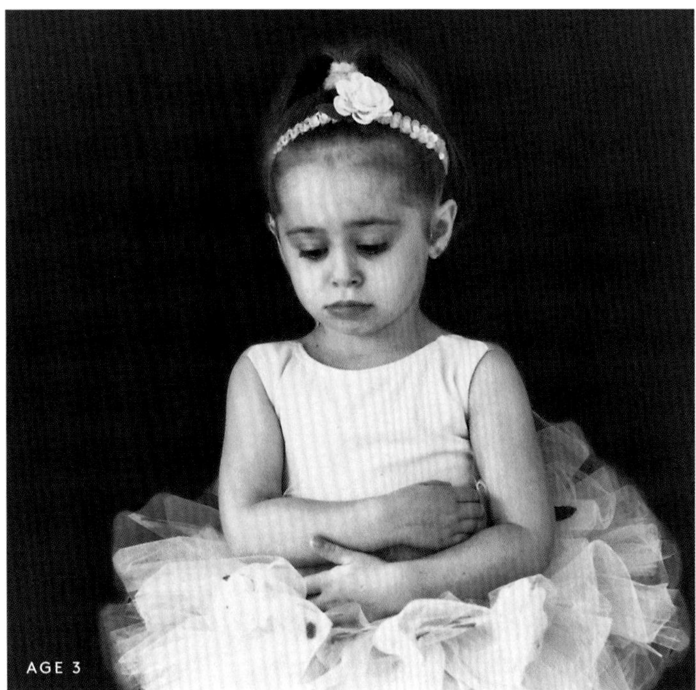

AGE 3

RYAN, AT 12: The nice thing about being a kid is that you don't have to worry about rent and mortgage stuff. I want to be a forensic detective. My advice to someone becoming a parent is have everything planned out. Don't just play it by ear. Have a job. Be married. Also, try to be there as much as the other parent so one won't be more important. Be your kid's friend. Don't try to be with them too much; give them space if they need it. But not too much. It's kind of confusing.

RYAN

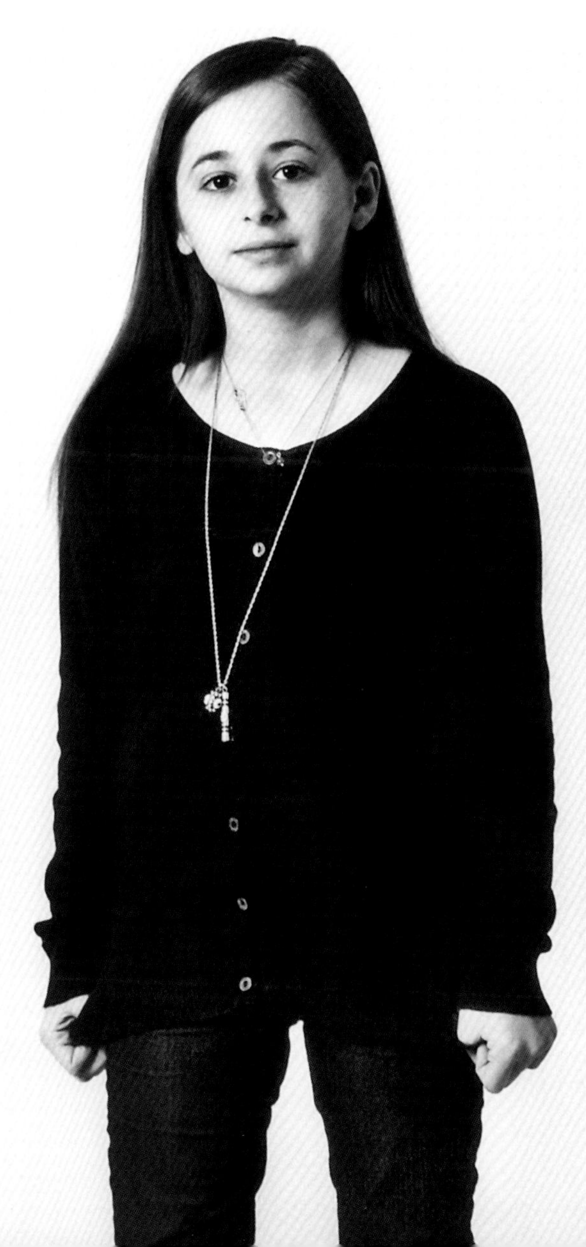

AGE 11

JONATHAN

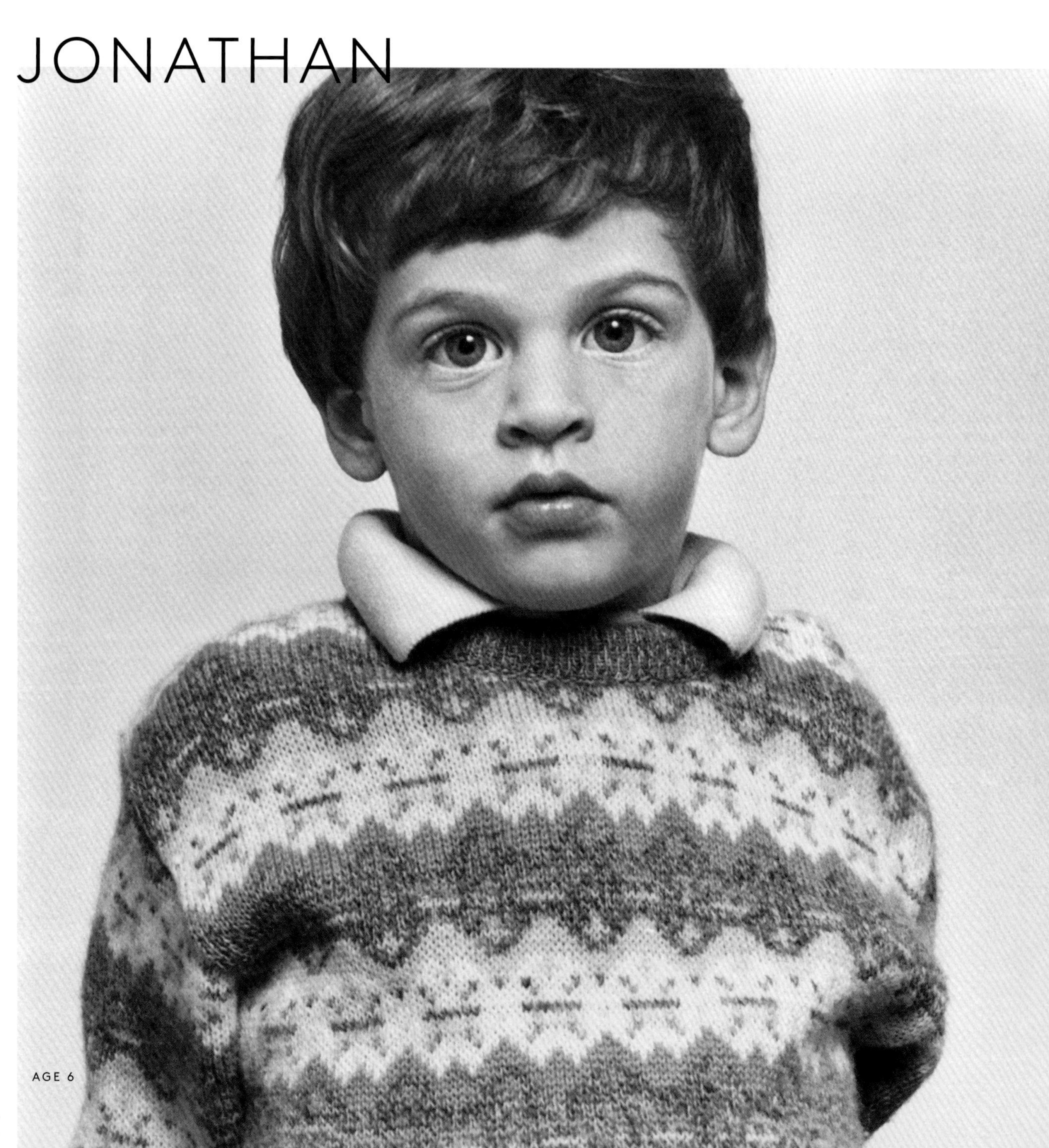

AGE 6

JONATHAN, AT 26: When you're a child, a day feels like a year. And a year feels like a lifetime. While I still feel like a kid, the clock seems to be moving more quickly these days. Then again, my clock may just be broken.

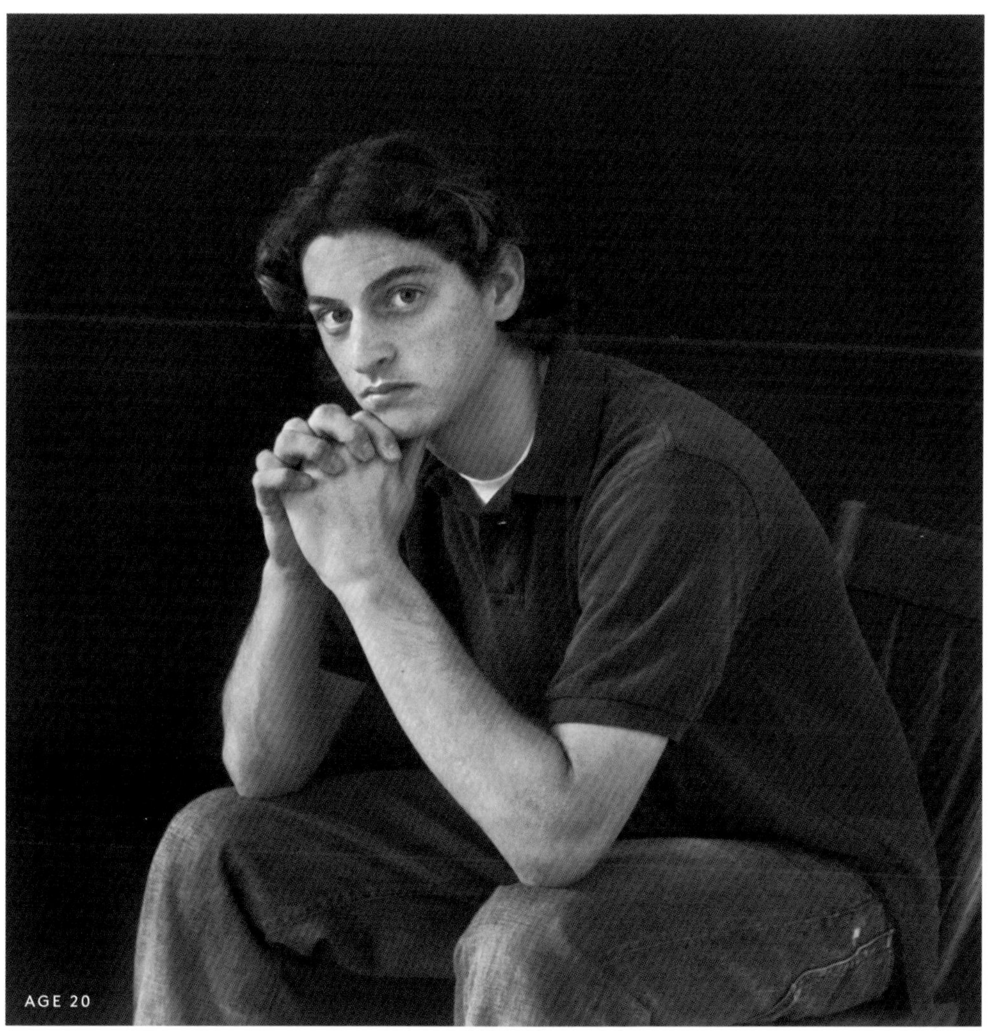
AGE 20

MOLLY, AT 16: It's hard thinking about the future, what you're going to do the rest of your life. Like right now, I'm beginning to look at colleges. I know what I want to do — I like music and I want a school that will build me up to be the best I can be. But what if I don't get in that school? Did I end up the way I thought I would? When I was little I wanted to be a nice person always and do my best in everything — that's the person I wanted to be. And that's the person I've become. My advice to parents: have your children treat each other as best friends; keep telling them that. And have them grow up without too much technology.

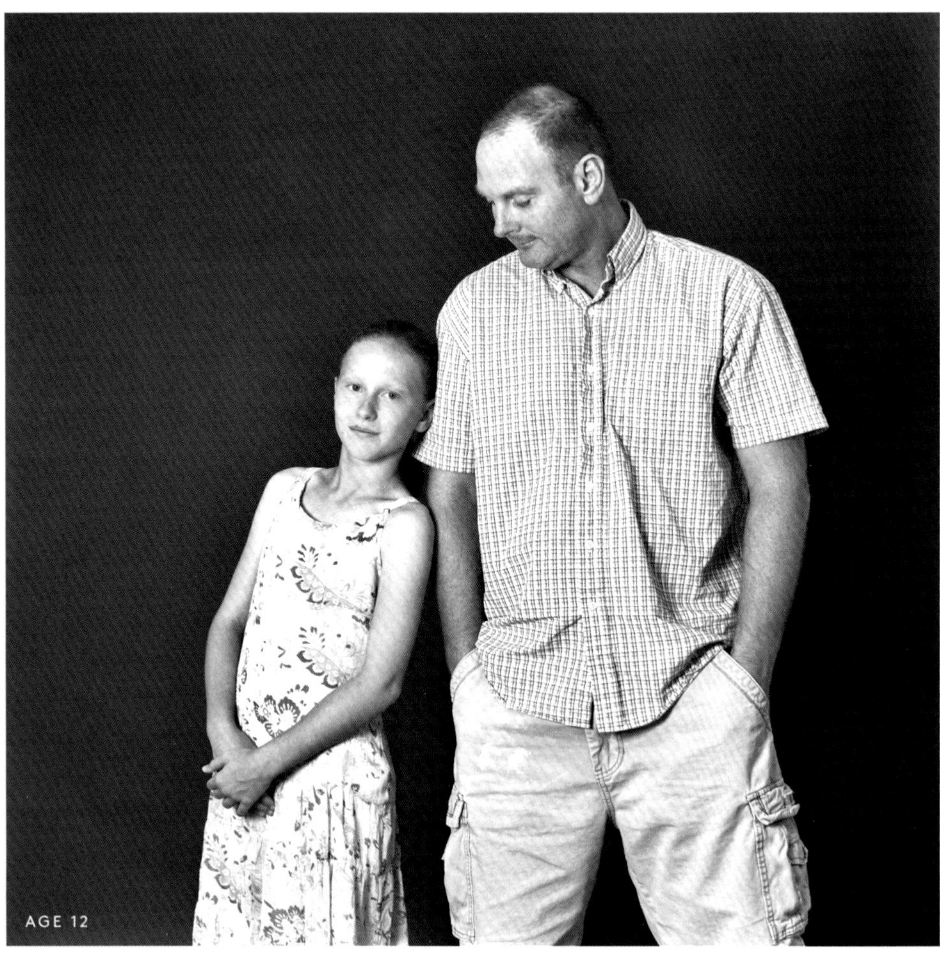
AGE 12

MOLLY

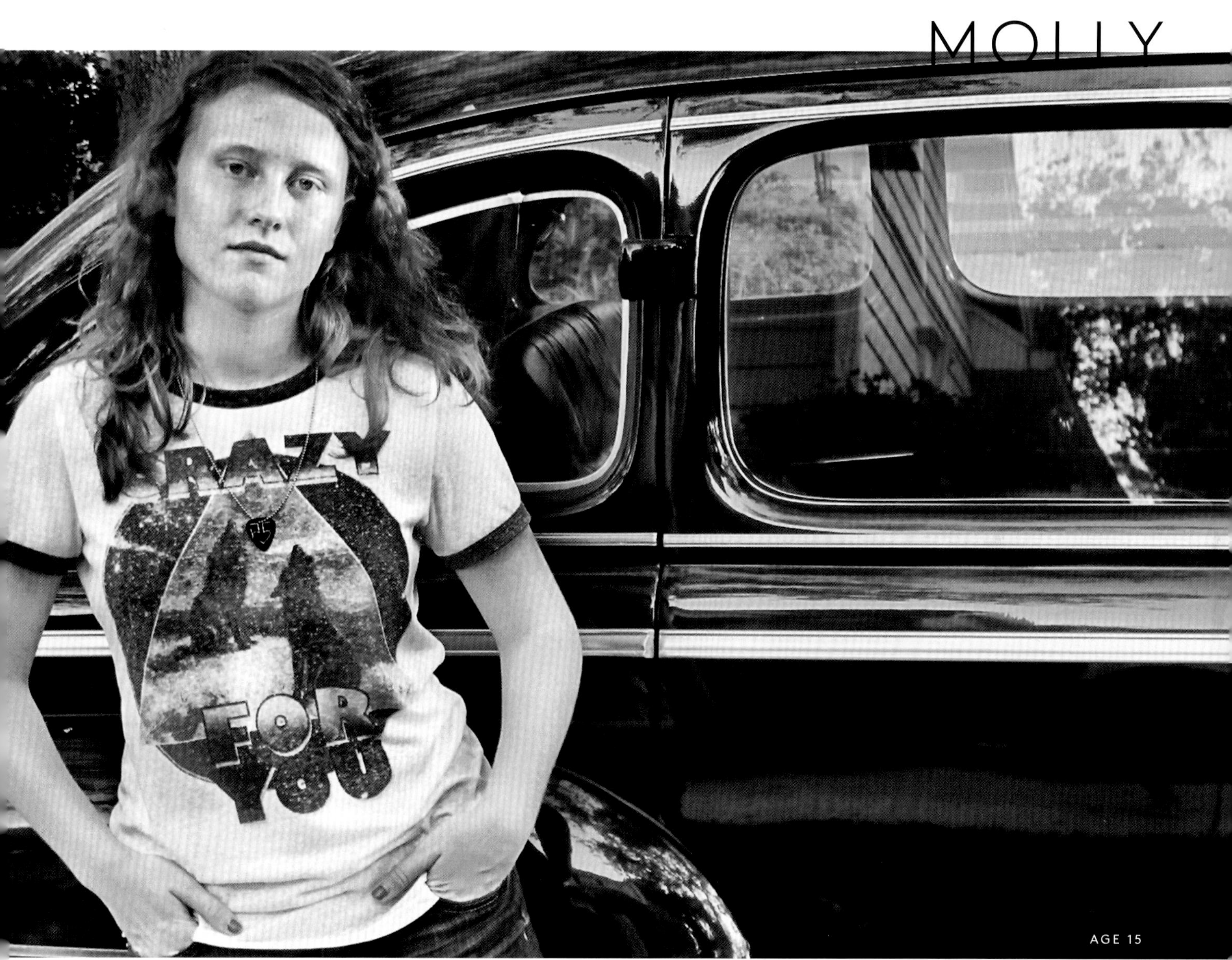

AGE 15

ETHAN, JONAH & ASHER

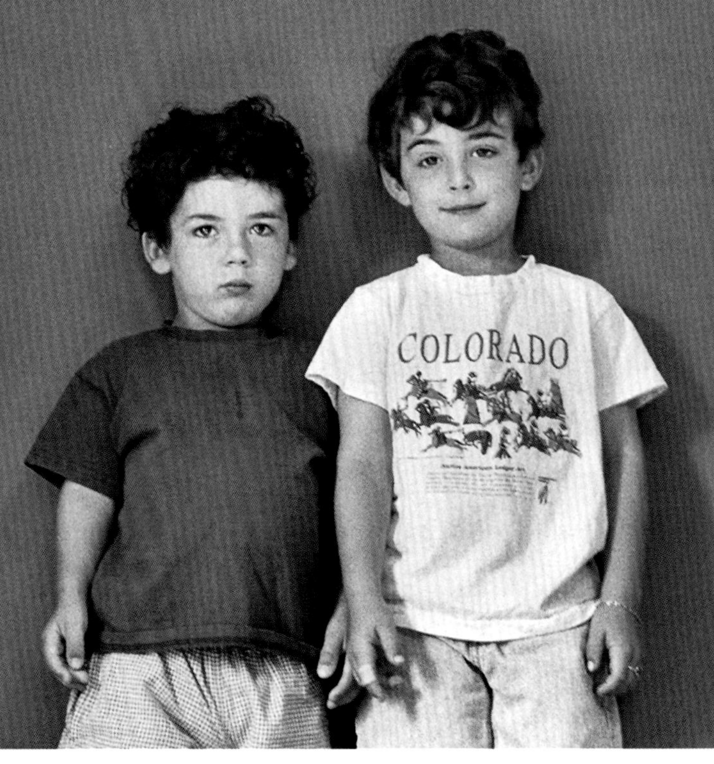

AGES 2 & 5

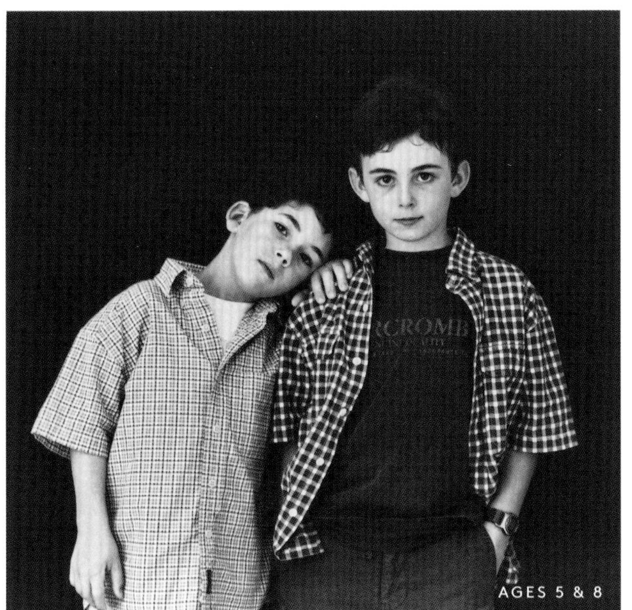
AGES 5 & 8

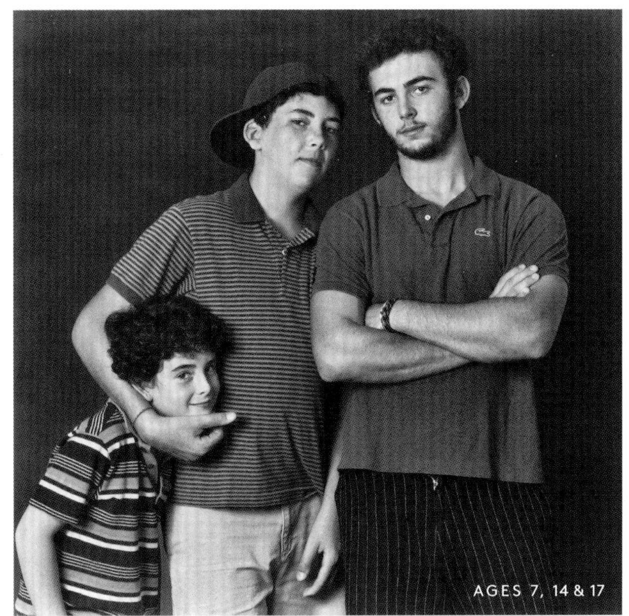
AGES 7, 14 & 17

ETHAN, ON THE LEFT IN FIRST TWO PHOTOS AND IN THE MIDDLE IN THE THIRD, AT 17: He's Jonah and I'm Ethan. In each picture, I take his place, I become him. We're alike. He's a role model. Even though I'm taller, I'm still his younger brother — I'm still leaning on him. And I never thought I'd have a little brother. I'm in the middle. I play both roles now. What's changed? I don't need my mommy as much. Well, not quite as much.

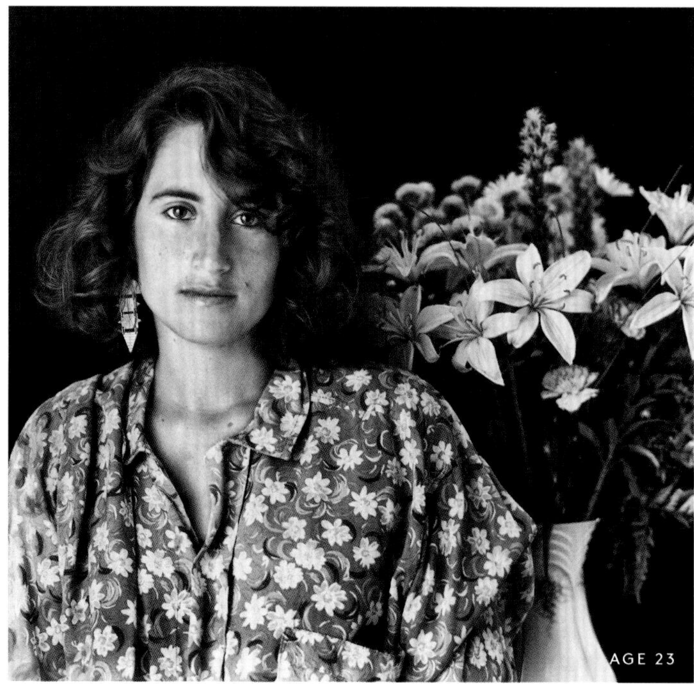

JENNIFER, THE DAUGHTER OF THE PHOTOGRAPHER, AT 45: In the first picture I'm young, naïve. I wasn't in business school yet, I was working in New York at Bloomingdale's, my first job out of college. Having fun. What has changed? I'm so far from where I was then. Not that much is the same, well, my love for my mother. In the first picture, I'm wearing her shirt and also her earrings... which I kept and still have. And in the second, her necklace, which I also still have. I'm surprised that it took me so long to get where I am now, doing work that I enjoy. I still have a long way to go career wise. I love this image of my daughter and me. It reminds me of my mother and myself.

JENNIFER & JULIA

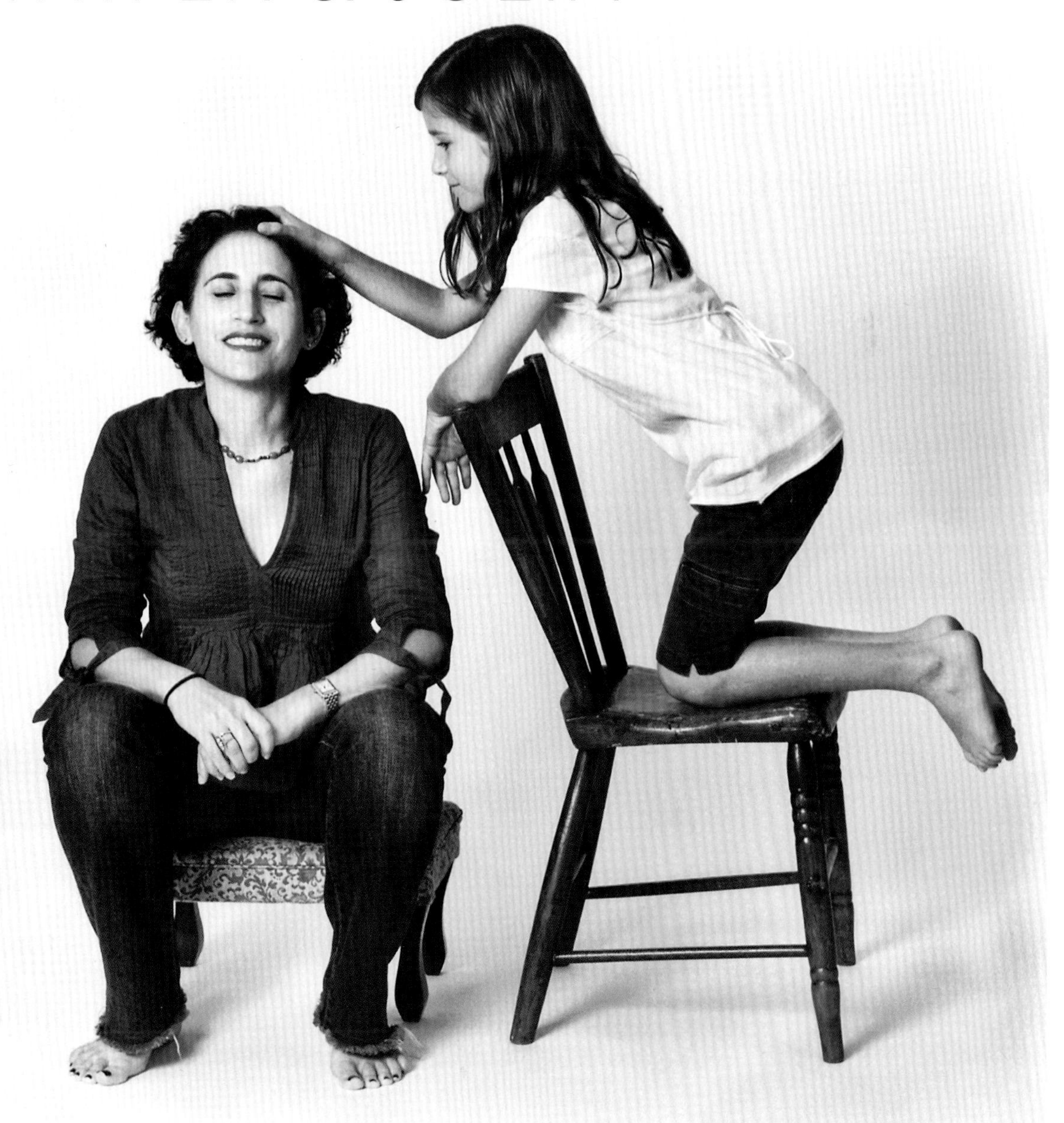

AGES 42 & 9

AUBREY & SARAH

AGES 4 & 6

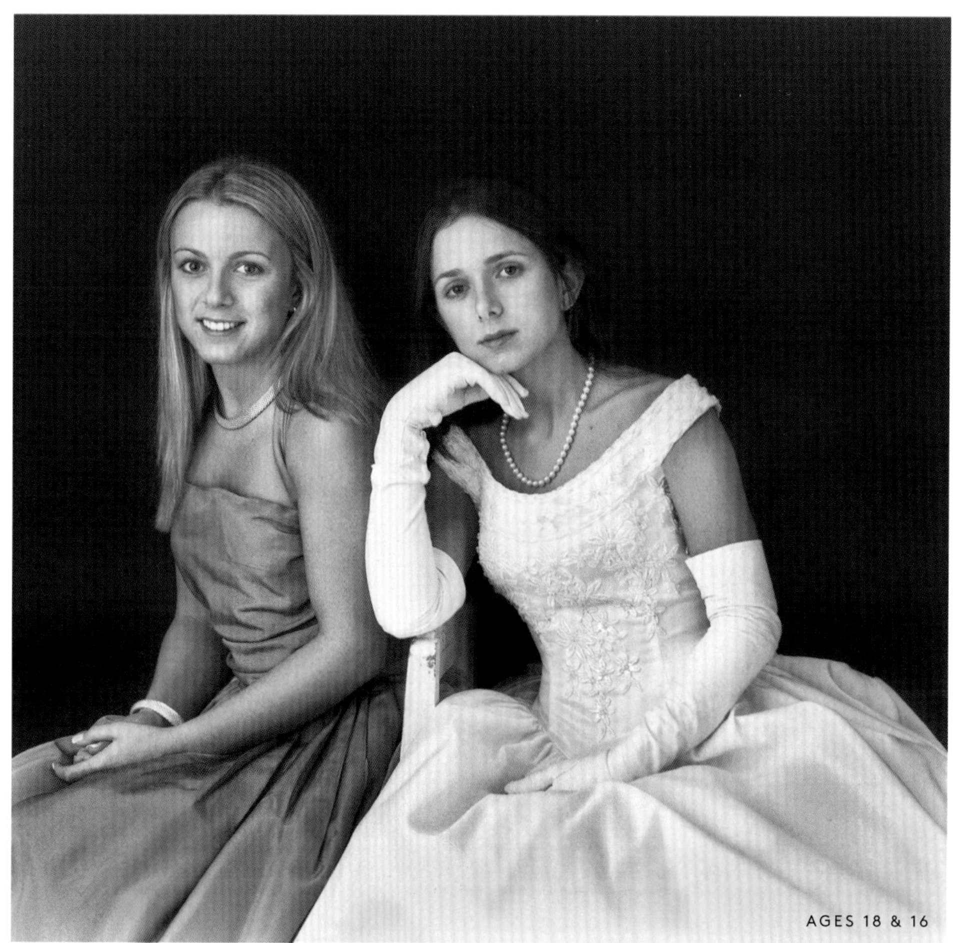

THEIR MOTHER: The girls had been invited to come to a birthday party dressed as mommies. I didn't realize that it was a tea party given by a group of religious people. The other girls came dressed demurely, white gloves. Then my girls, dressed for a nightclub, came in: cut-down bridesmaids' dresses, rhinestone earrings. The other kids were heartbroken.

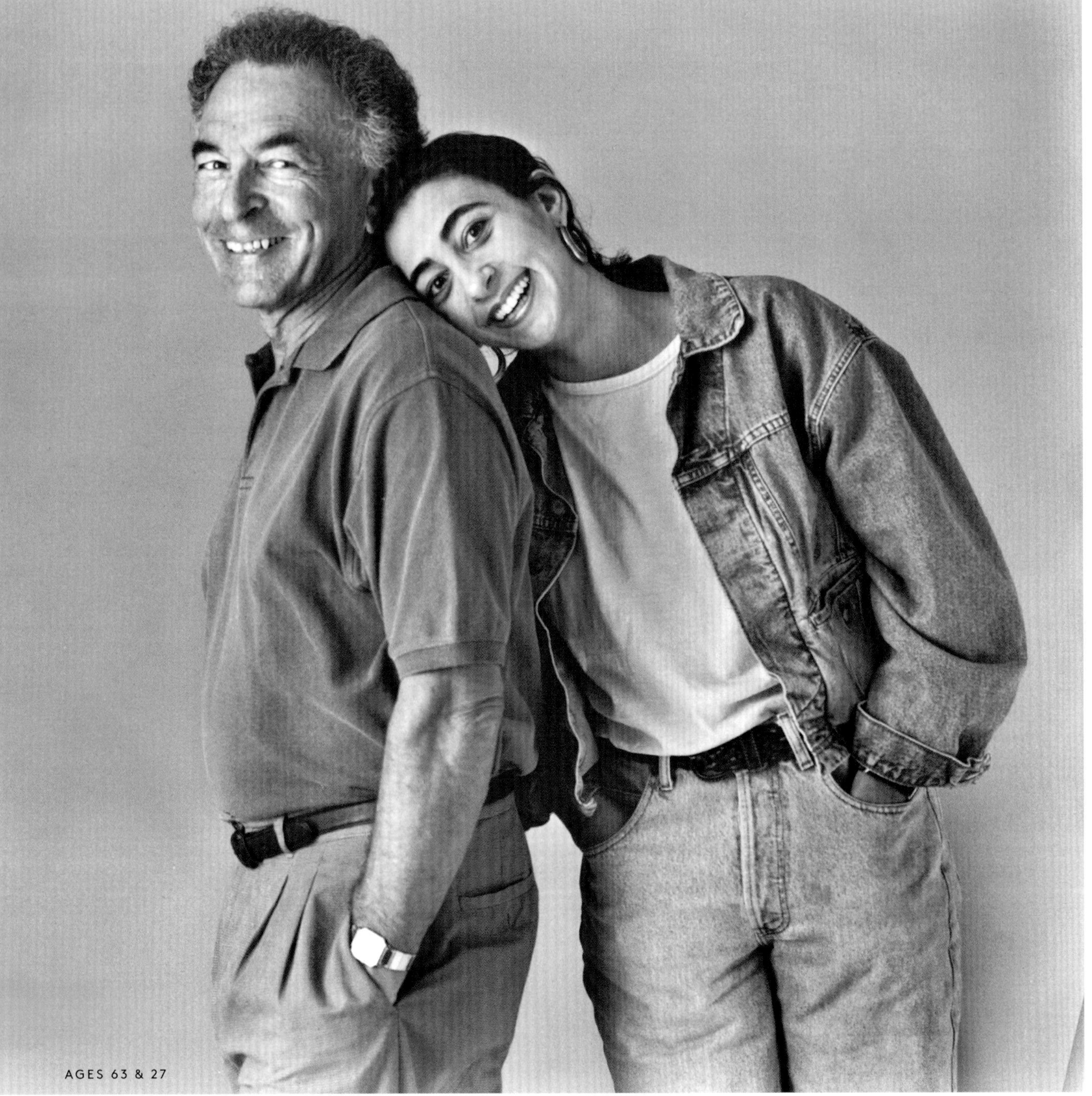

AGES 63 & 27

JOAN, AT 45: All my childhood, at every meal, I would eat quickly and go sit on my dad's lap; maybe he would be just one-third of the way done. He would rub my back. It never bothered him. **BERNIE:** I'm put off by my aging — but I have the beauty of my grandson, who looks like me. That makes me feel good. **JOAN:** I'm still the baby and now Max is my baby.

BERNIE, JOAN & MAX

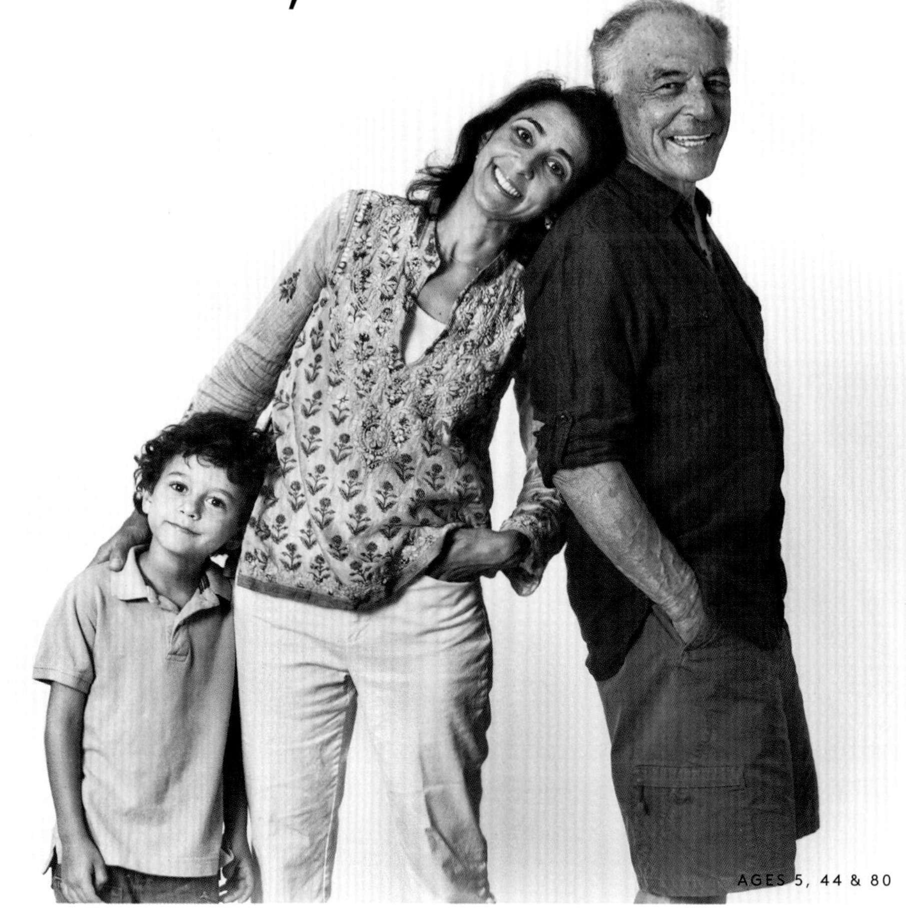

AGES 5, 44 & 80

ALEXANDRA & FRANKIE

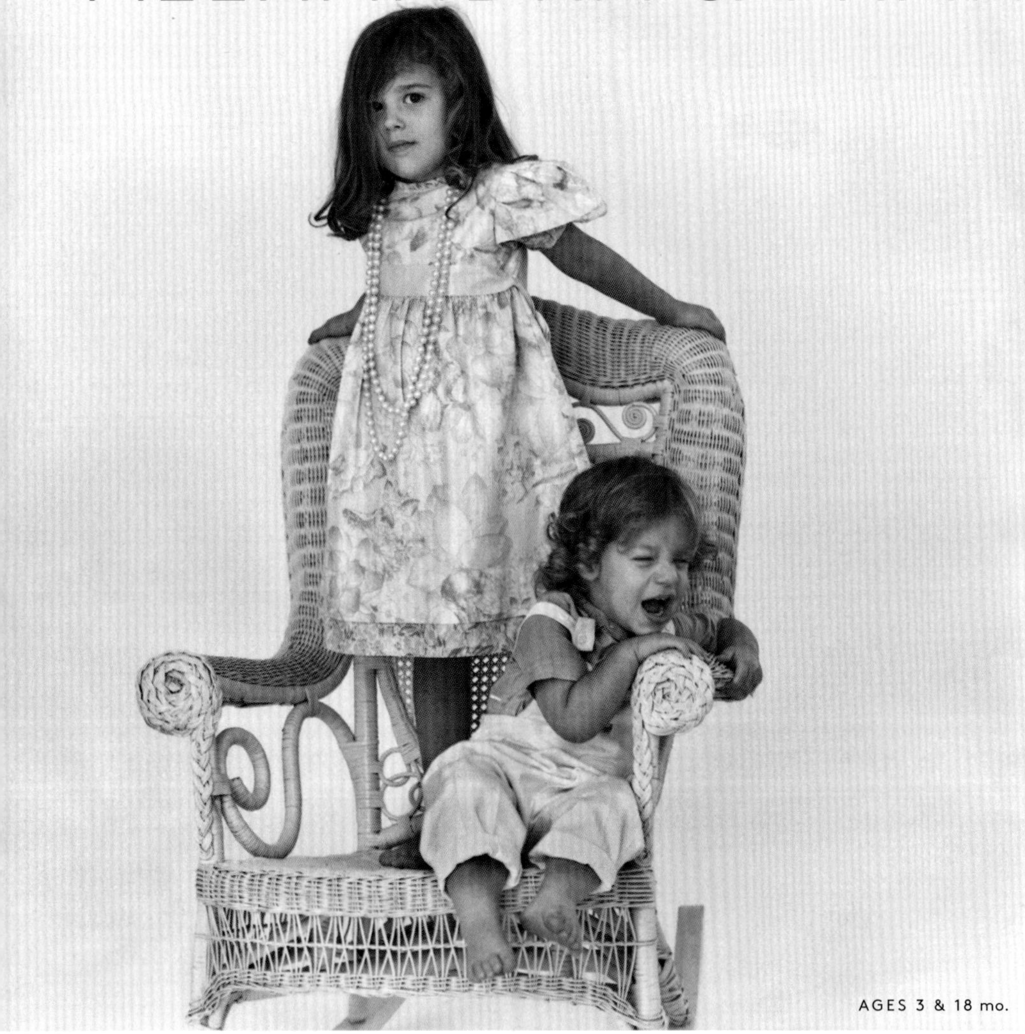

AGES 3 & 18 mo.

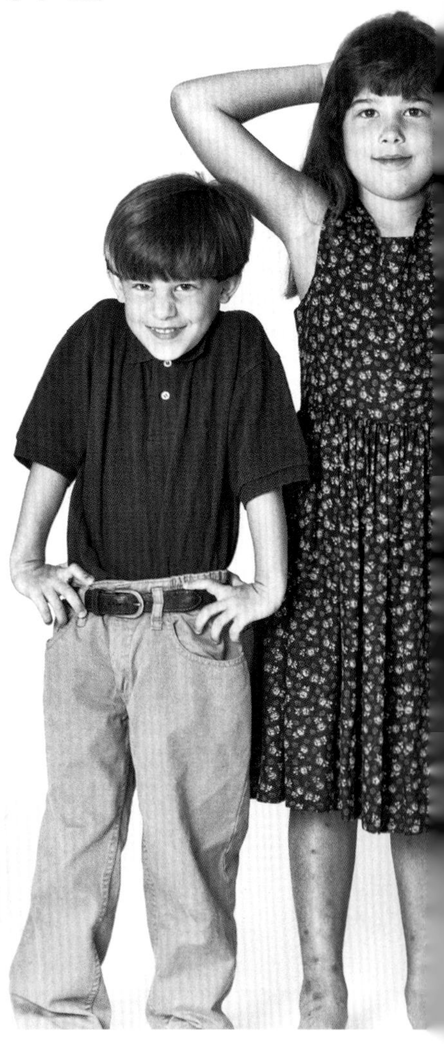

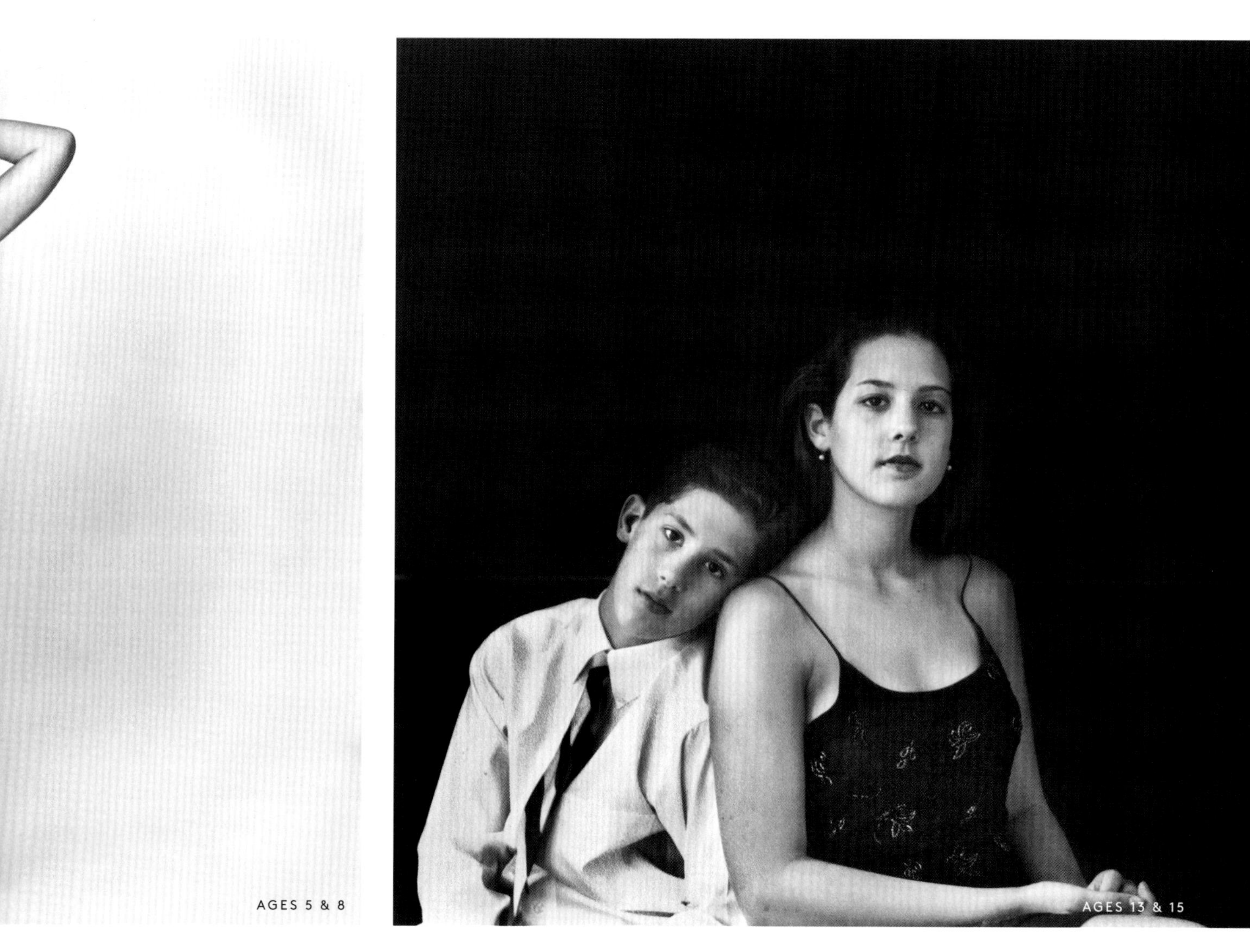

AGES 5 & 8

AGES 13 & 15

ALEXANDRA, AT 24: I would say when you become a parent, try to enjoy even the sleepless nights and sacrifices that every person has to make when they become a parent, because many people in the world aren't able to have kids of their own.

ALISON

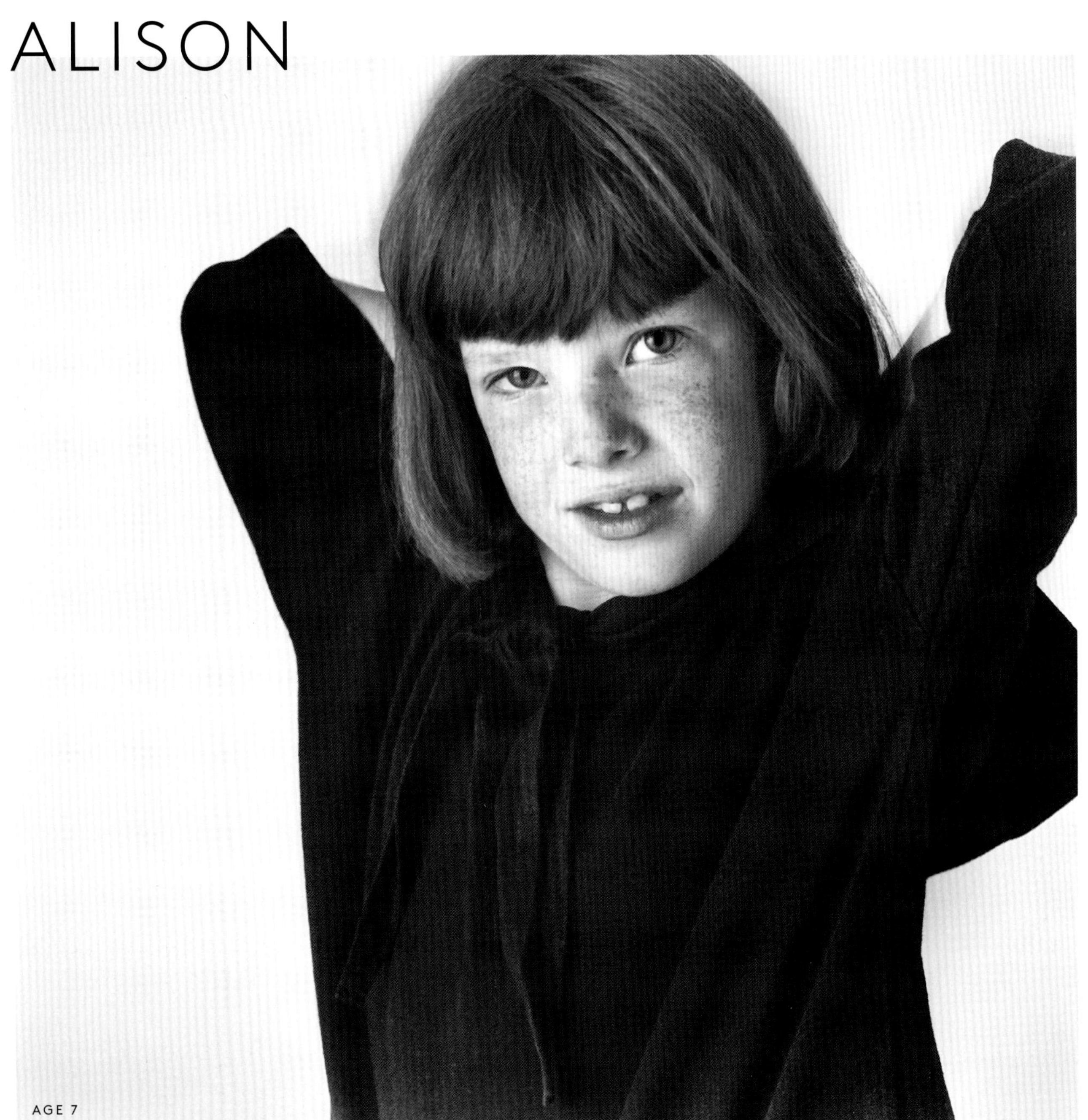

AGE 7

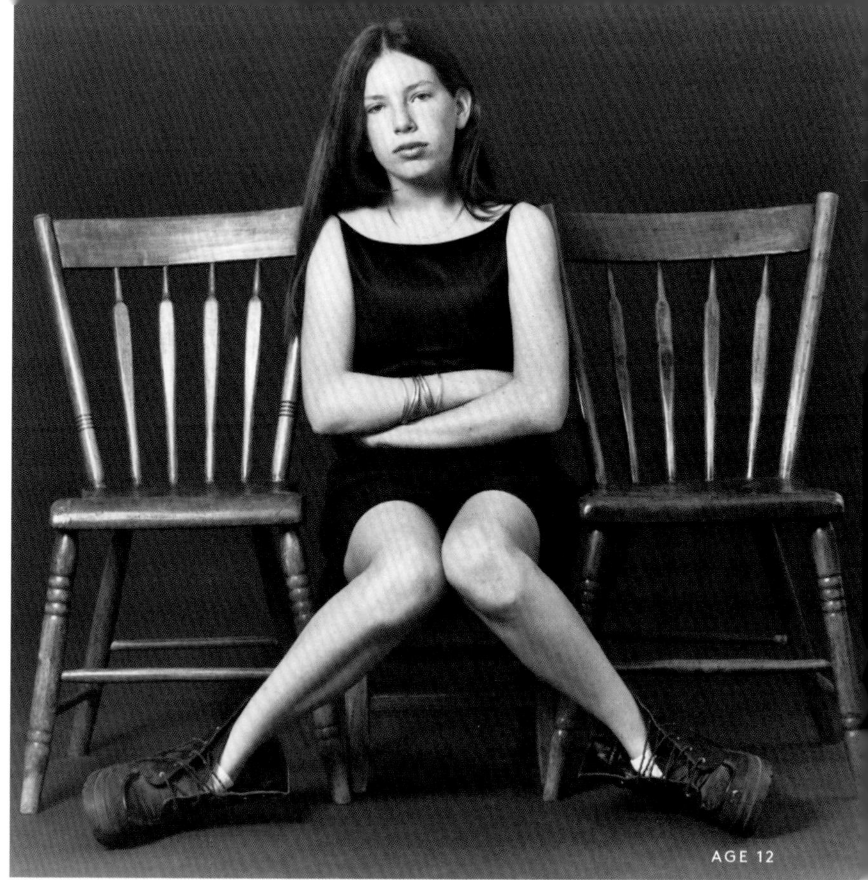

ALISON, AT 25: I felt I would never grow older. I couldn't imagine a time when I would be living on my own and having my own life. Now I think, slow down—my own life, bills to pay, the real world. I wear my heart on my sleeve. There are no secrets about how I'm feeling. In the second picture I would say I was happiest when with my friends; now, at twenty-five, I would say it's with my family. I'm very sentimental. I've had such a good life; I like to feel grateful.

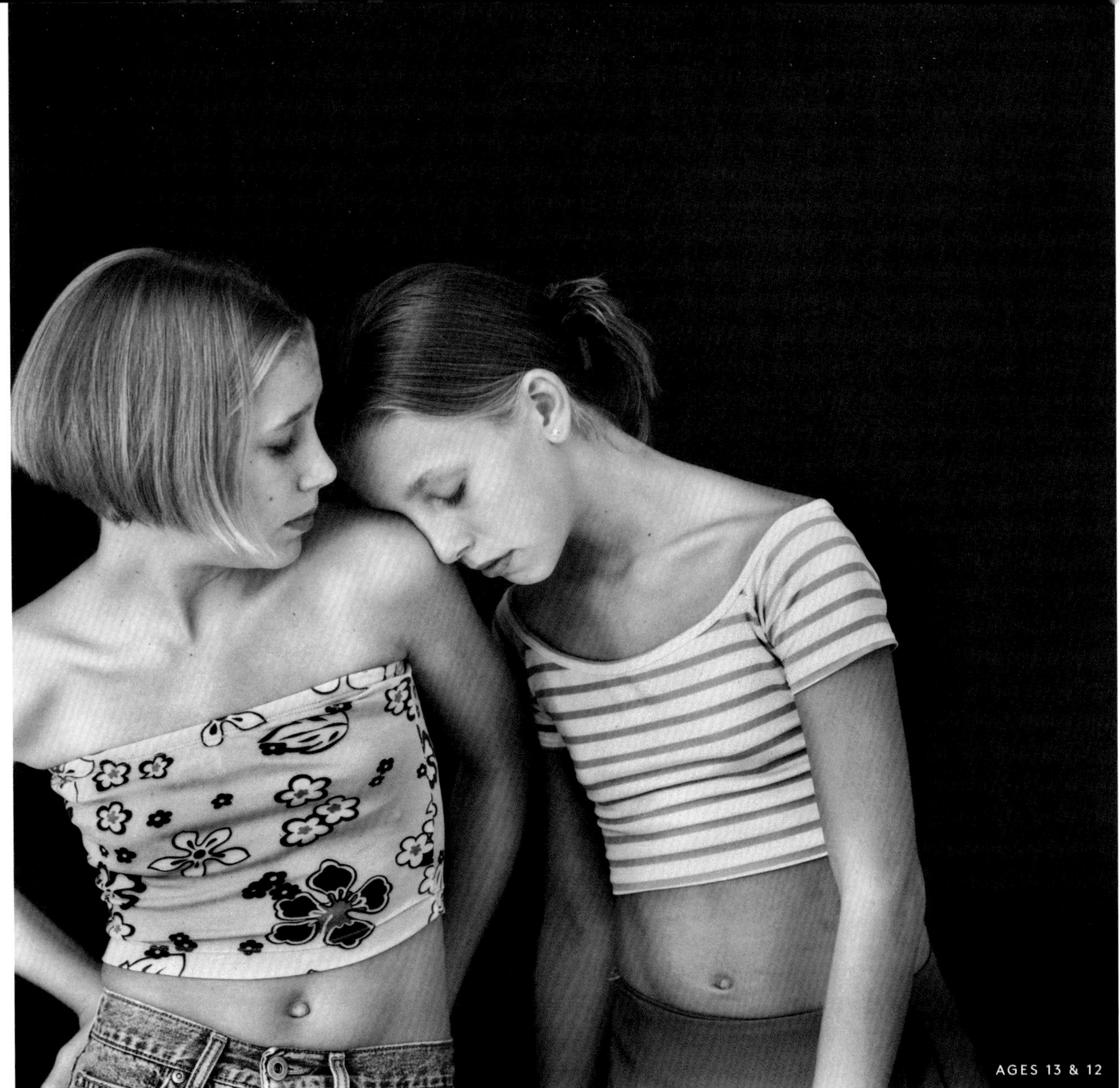

KARINA, AT 23: I feel it important to say that more now than ever I consider my sister my best friend. When I consider advice to future parents I would say take some time every week to do something new together as a family. And it's okay if your kid falls, just as long as you show them how to pick themselves back up.

ALEXI & KARINA

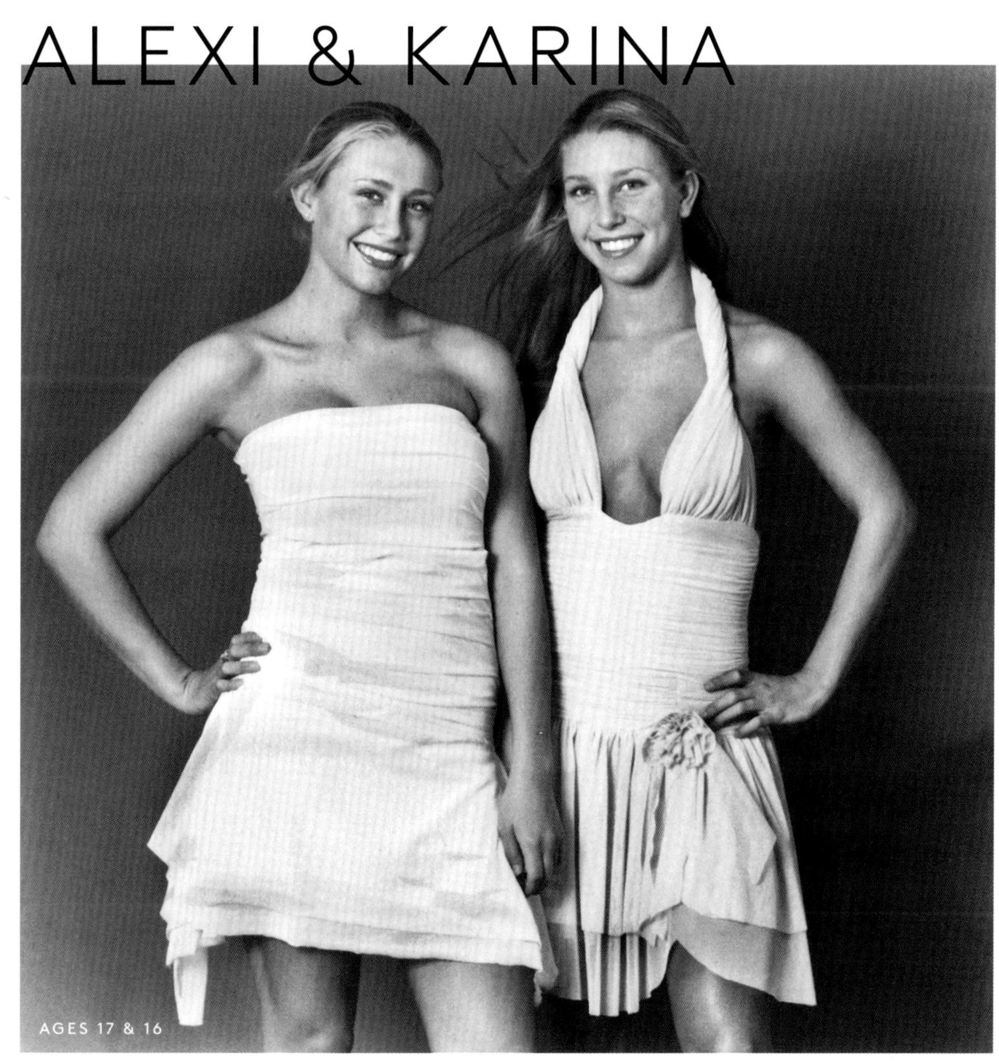

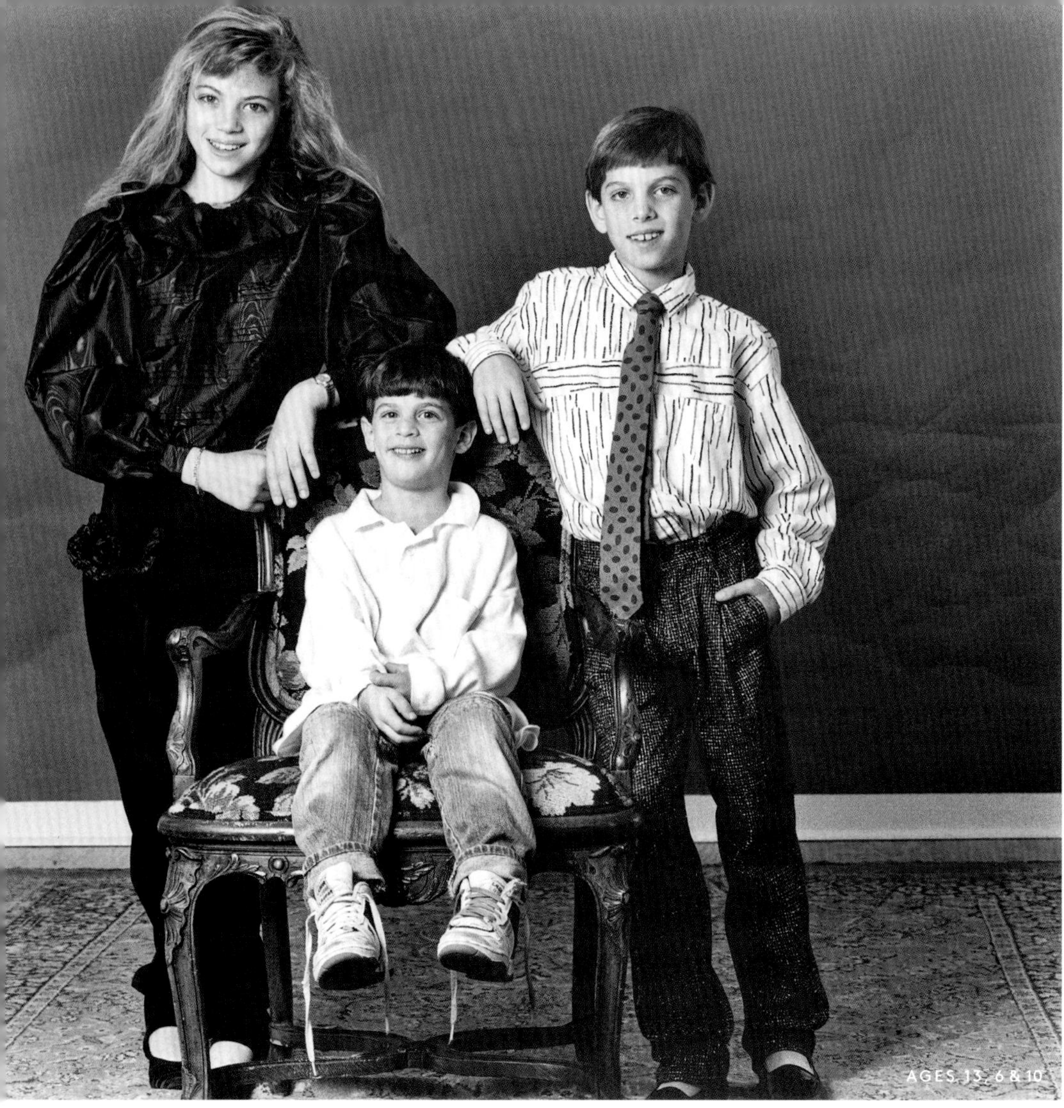

JONATHAN, AT 26: I don't remember much of the shoot; however, I'm confident it went a little something like this: my brother tries to hurt me, my sister comes to my rescue, a fight ensues between the two of them, my sister wins the physical battle, my brother the emotional. I'm thoroughly entertained.

LAUREN, DAVID & JONATHAN

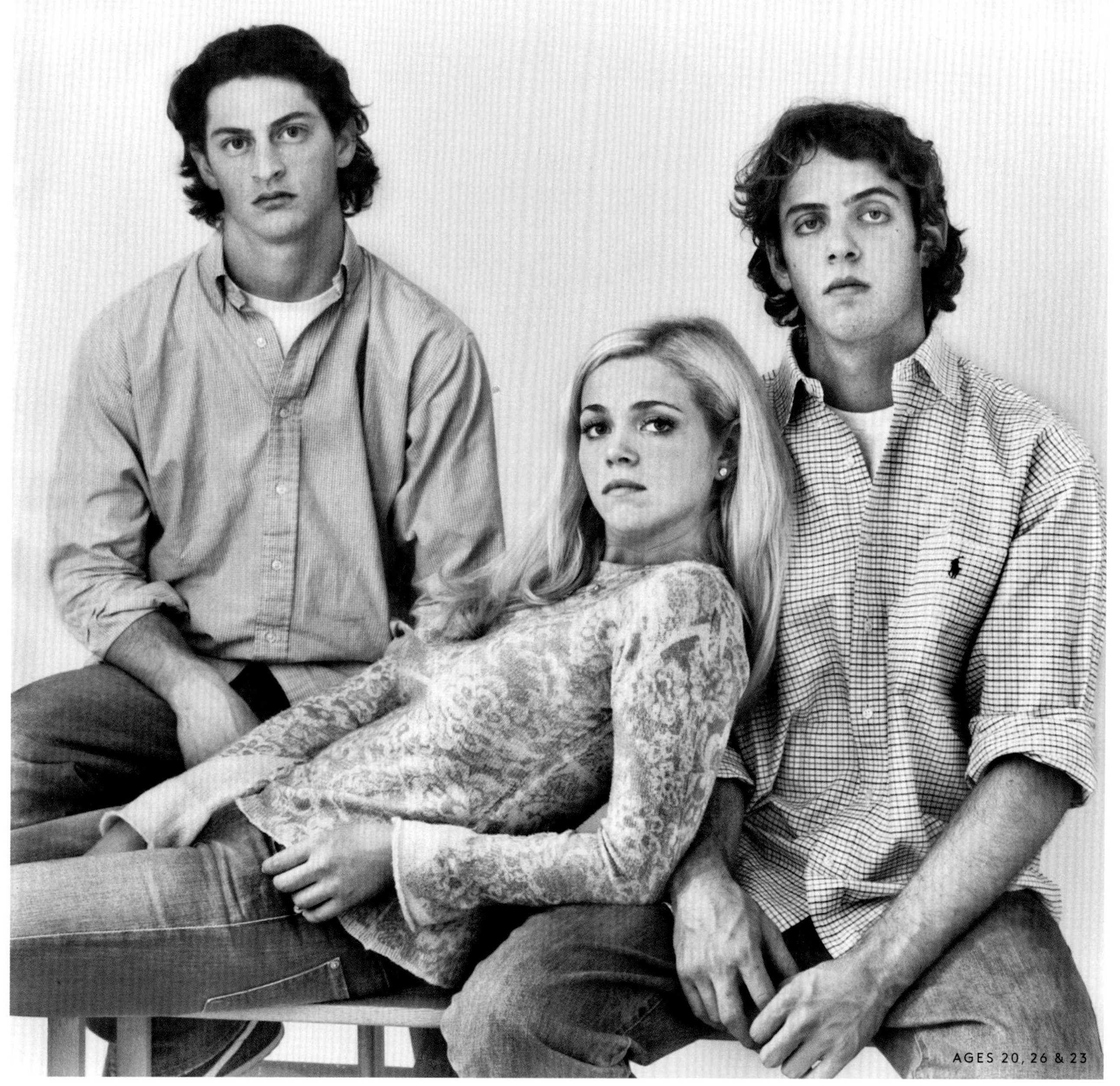

AGES 20, 26 & 23

STEVEN & DAVID

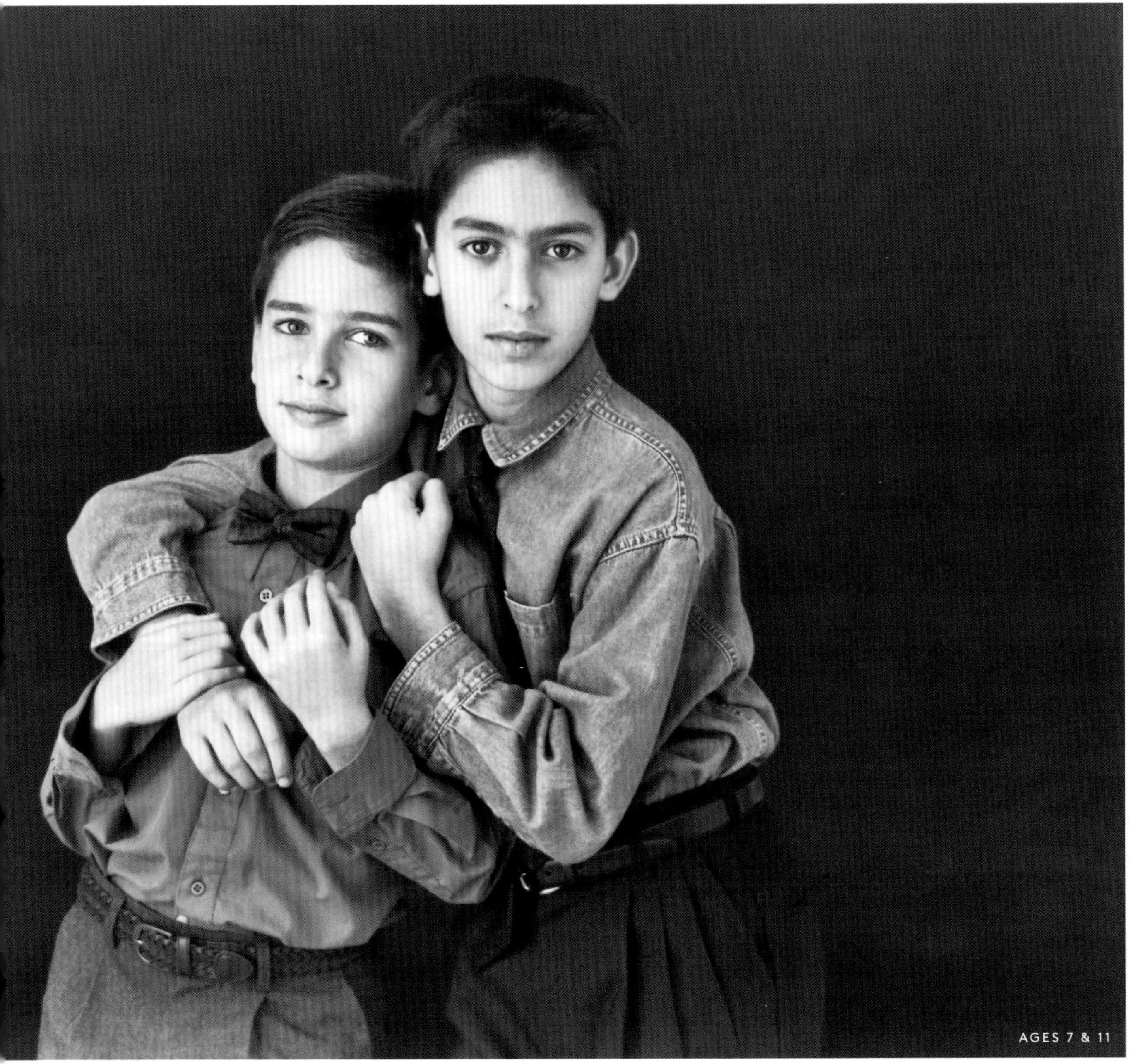

AGES 7 & 11

DAVID, ON RIGHT, AT 22: The pictures force me to dwell on the notion that we are different people at all points of our lives and all those different people make up the person we are today. Every time I really look at them, I am forced to let out a long sigh, as my mind becomes cluttered with feeling and memories no longer relevant, but for some reason still within me.

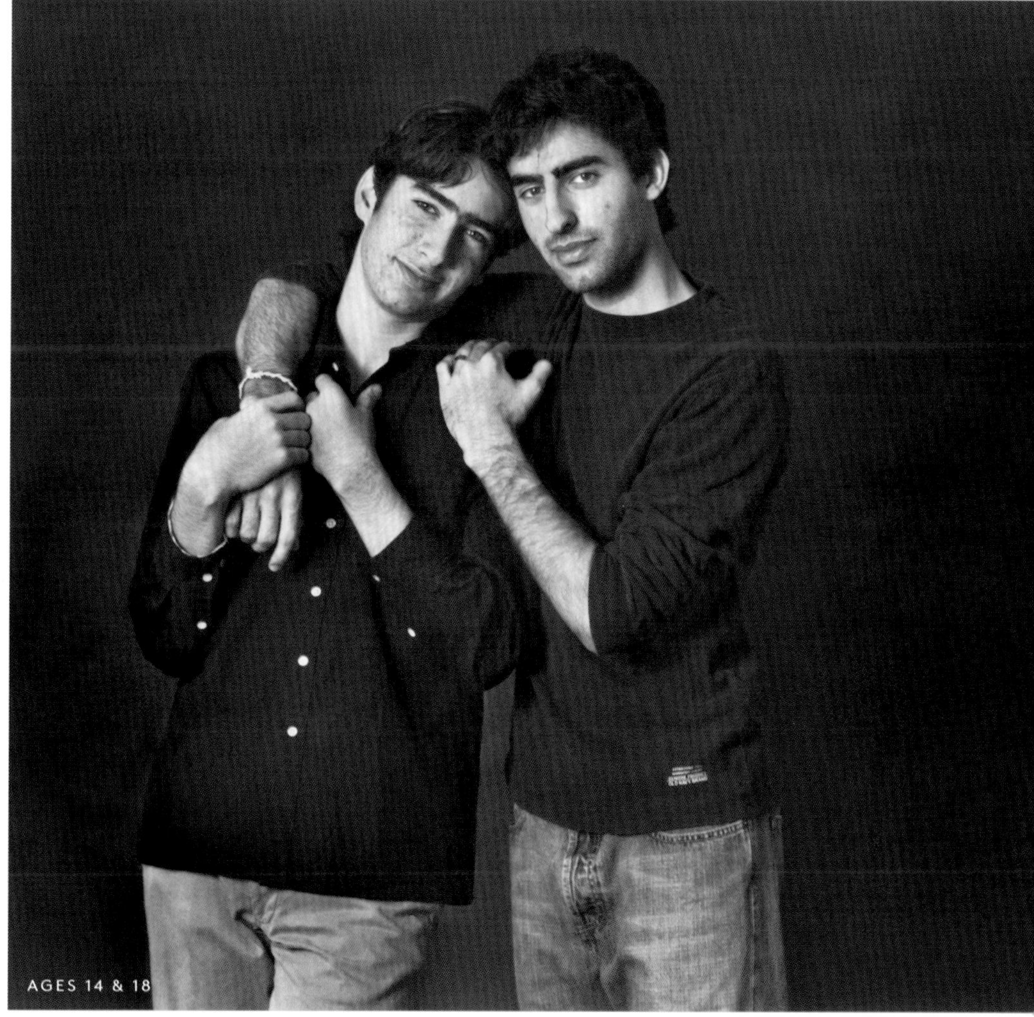

AGES 14 & 18

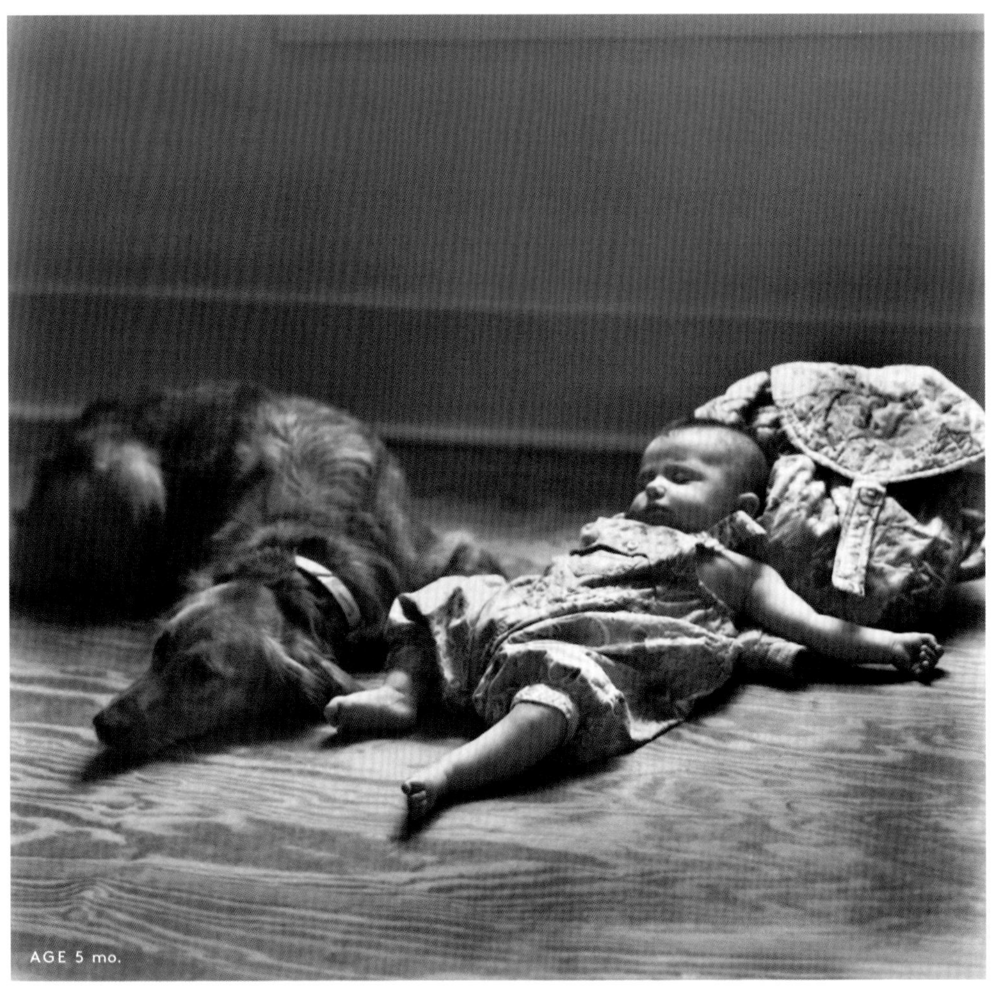

SOPHIE, AT 12: If you enjoy childhood, it goes by fast; if you're miserable you feel like it will never end.

SOPHIE

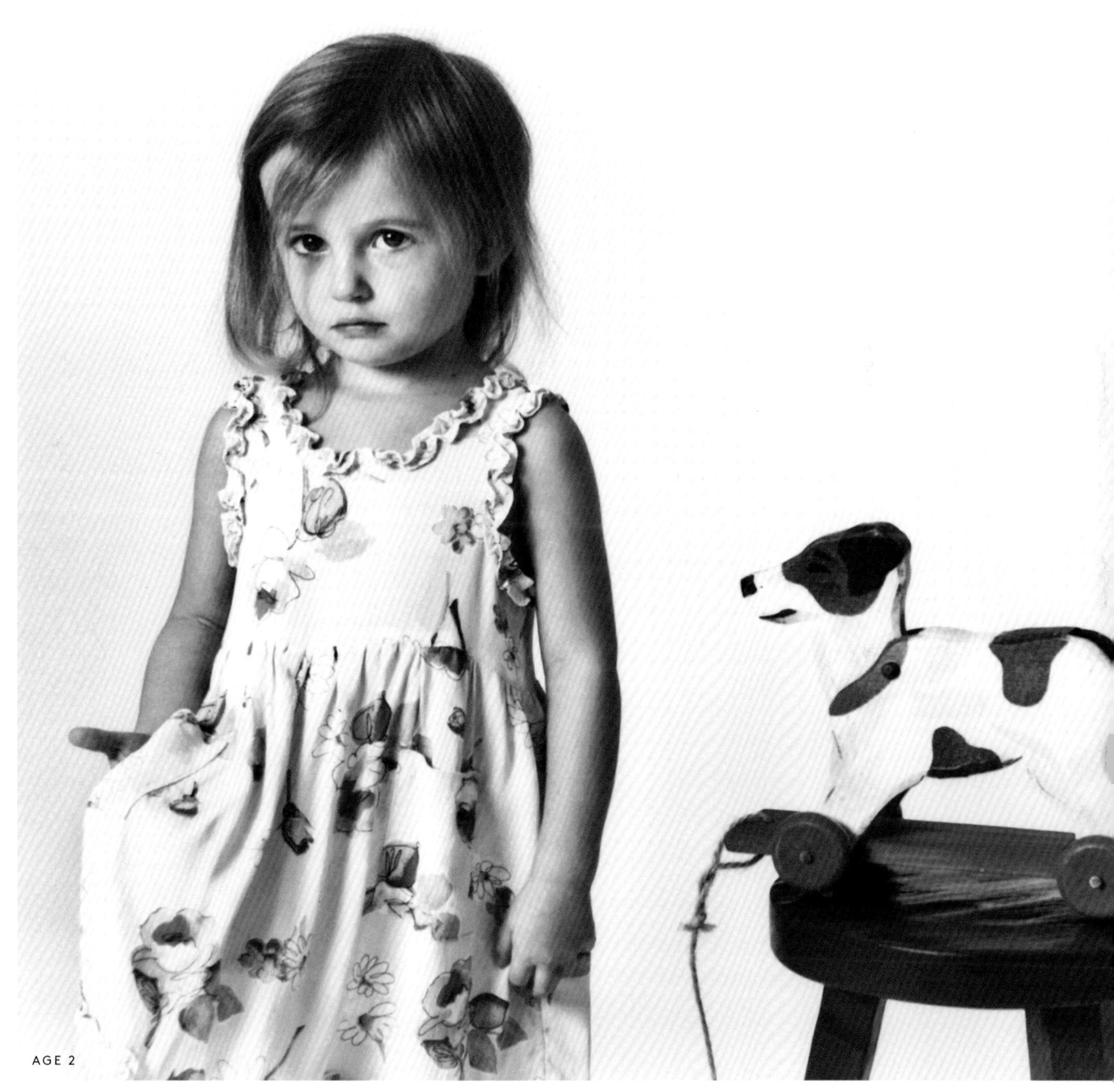

AGE 2

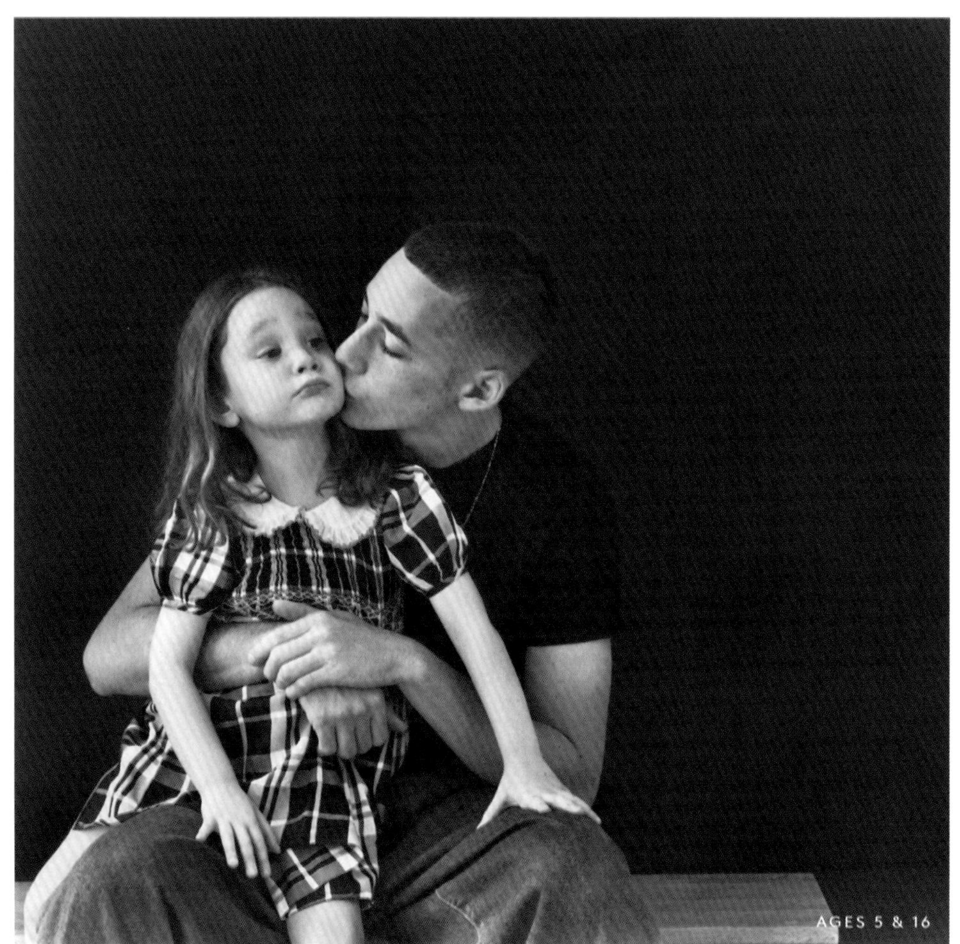

AGES 5 & 16

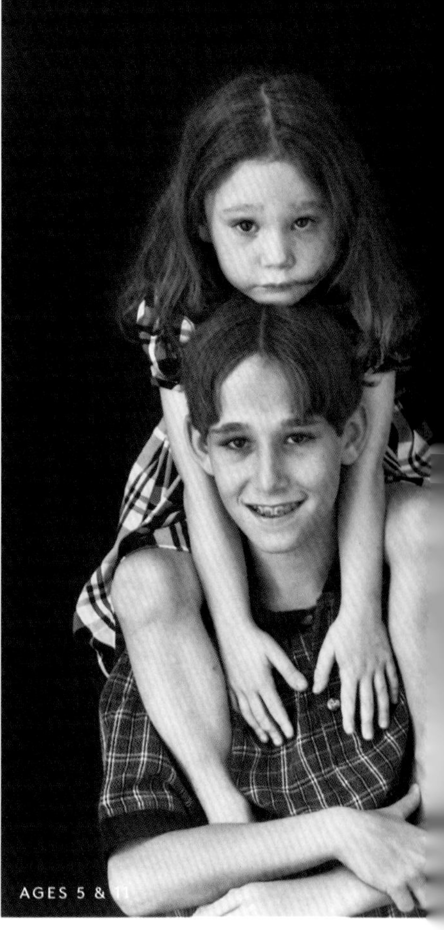

AGES 5 & 11

LEAH & BROTHERS

THEIR MOTHER: The wisdom is: "Stop. Look." My mom was always at the kitchen sink, dusting the corners; my grandmother was scalding the chicken, plucking the feathers. I think they missed it. Leah has the gift of three older brothers. They are a constant protection in her life and no matter what, she'll have that.

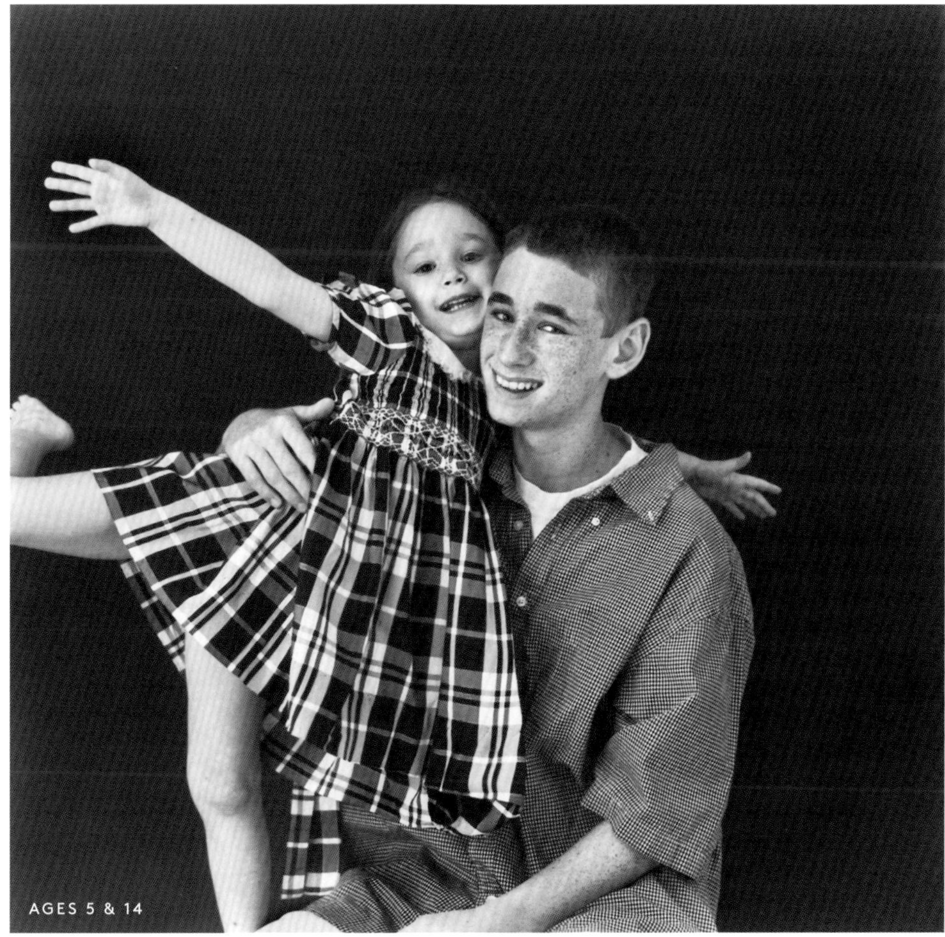

AGES 5 & 14

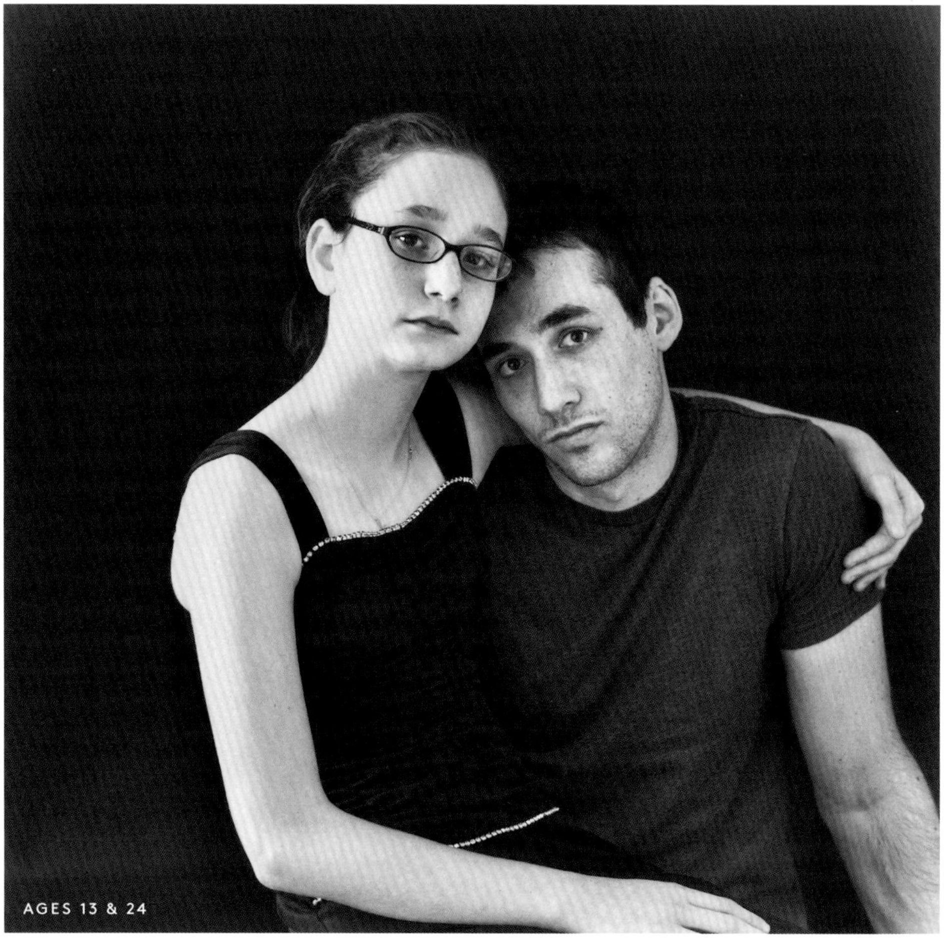

AGES 13 & 24

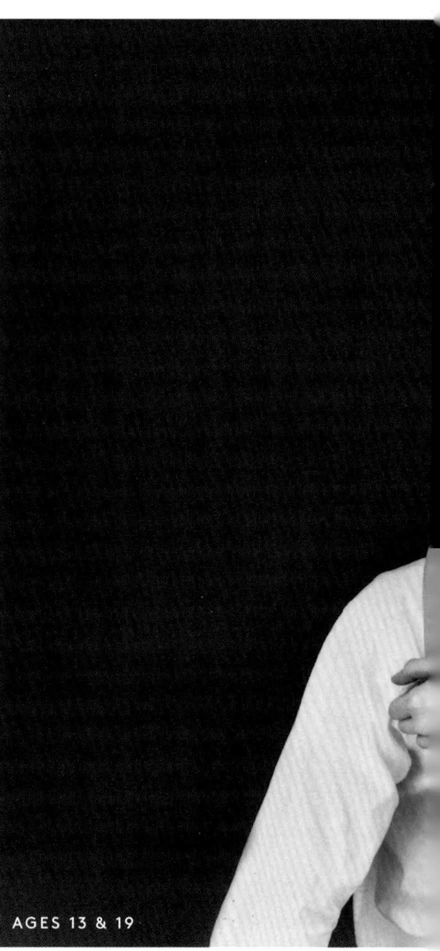

AGES 13 & 19

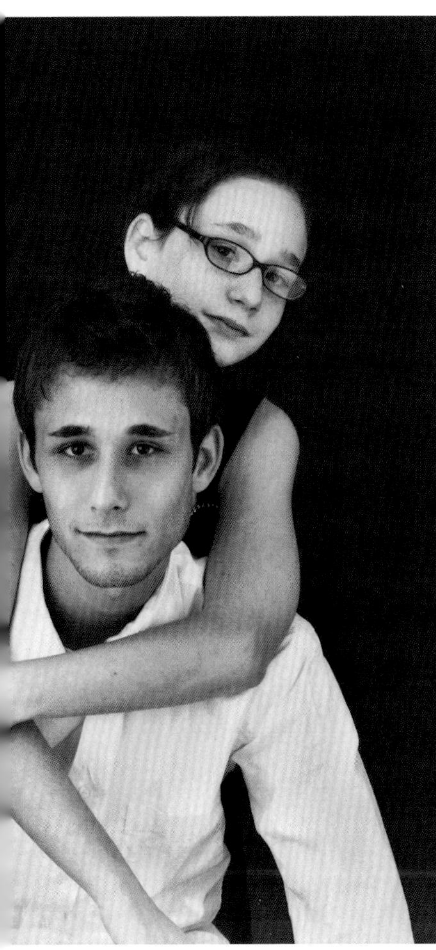

LEAH, AT 15: I was always happiest when I was with my brothers. It's the same now. I've always been a fun-loving girl. I'm adventurous; I like to get lost on purpose. I think about my life in the future: what I can do now to make it better.

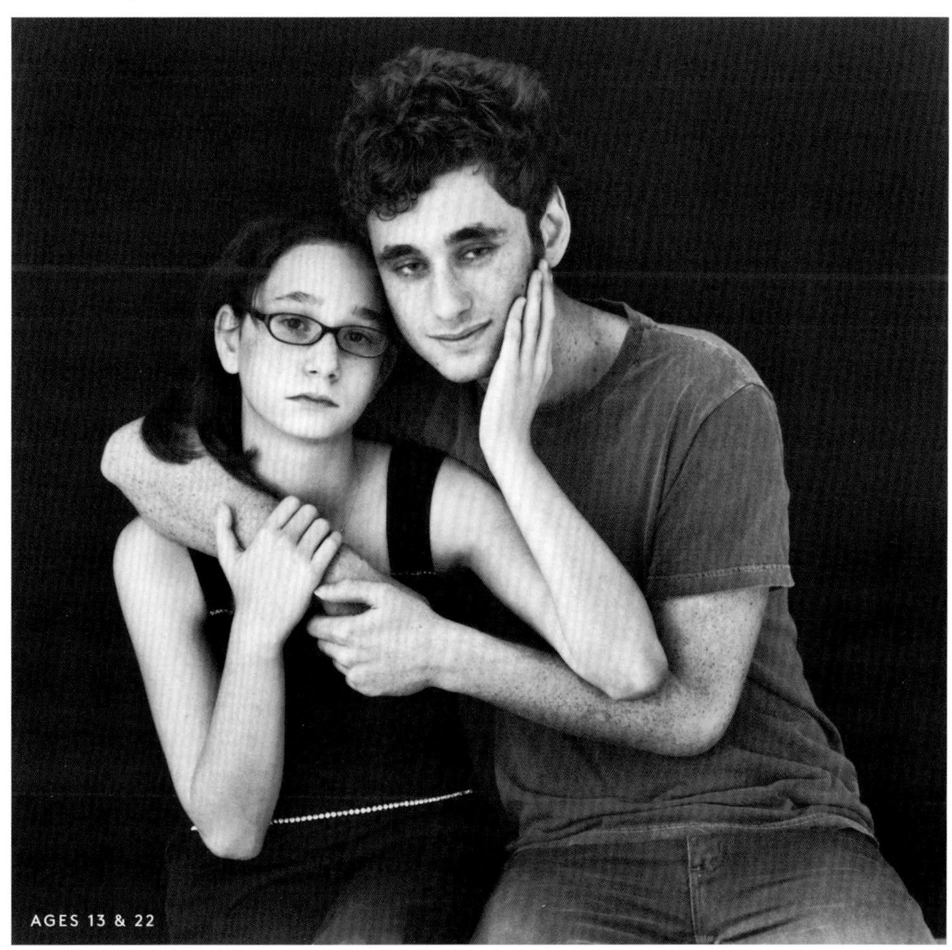

AGES 13 & 22

DANIELLE

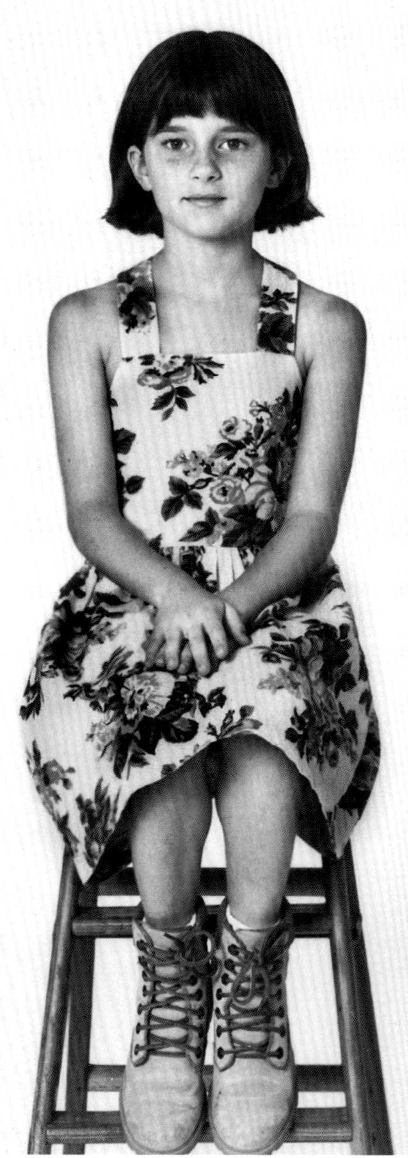

AGE 9

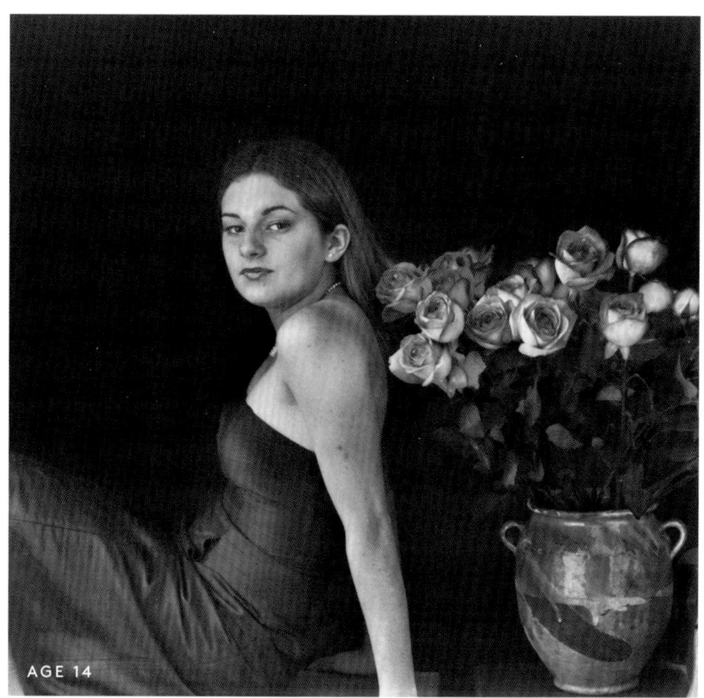
AGE 14

DANIELLE, AT 25: In childhood you have all the time in the world, and there's always so much support for you. What's hard is always trying to get to that next step. Its easier in adulthood to know that where you're at is a good place. I always wanted to make it to New York, which is where I currently live. I'm more career oriented than I had expected, and love working hard. When I'm not working, I'm an avid trapeze artist. I'm closer with my brother than I thought I would be — we live together! My mom strongly believed that having a full schedule meant I couldn't get myself in any trouble. Even now, I get a bit nervous when I have any downtime. I'm always on the go. My parents' philosophy was to let us do whatever we enjoyed doing, and take responsibility for ourselves at a pretty young age.

RACHEL & JOHN

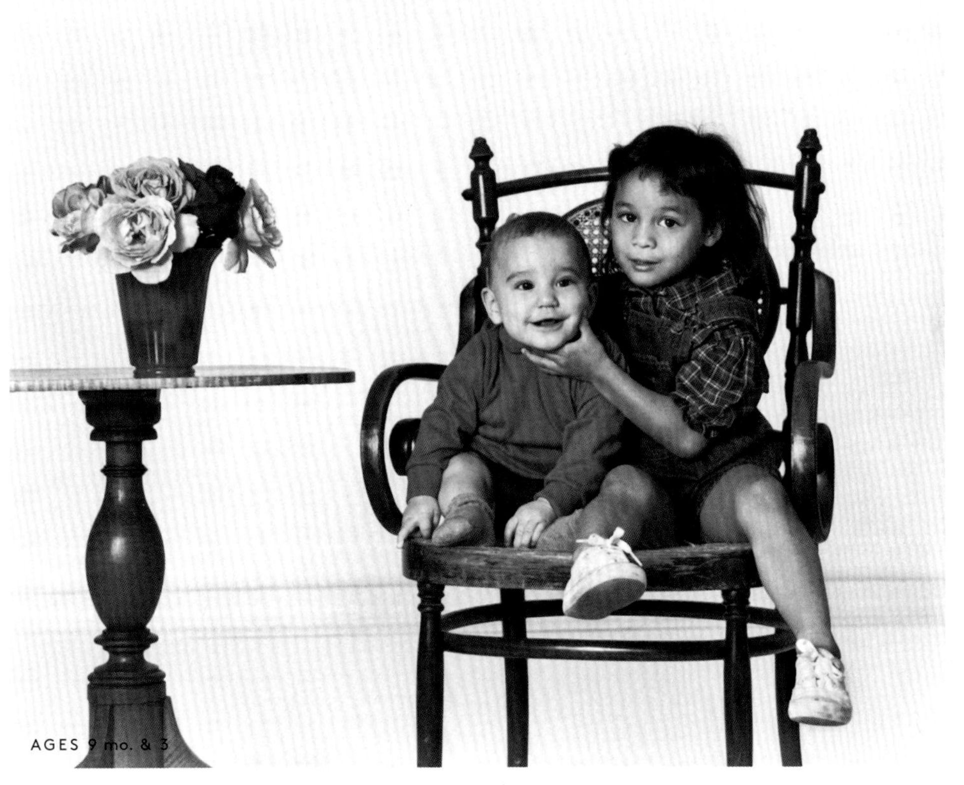
AGES 9 mo. & 3

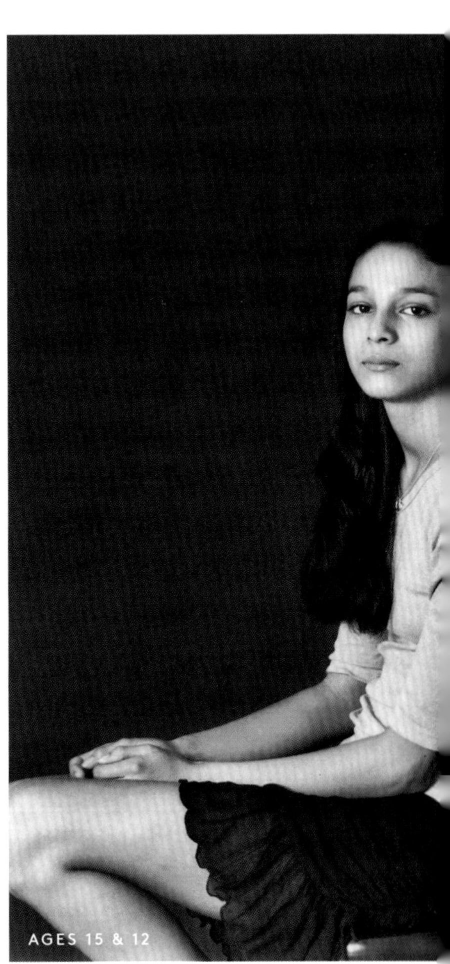
AGES 15 & 12

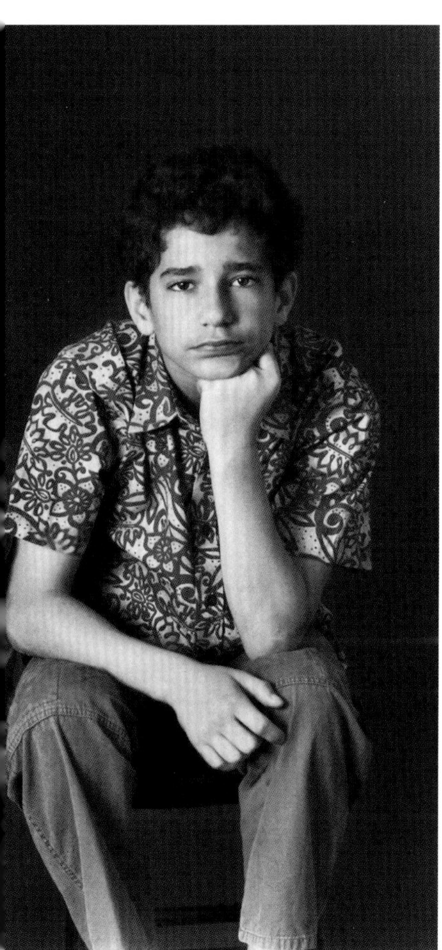

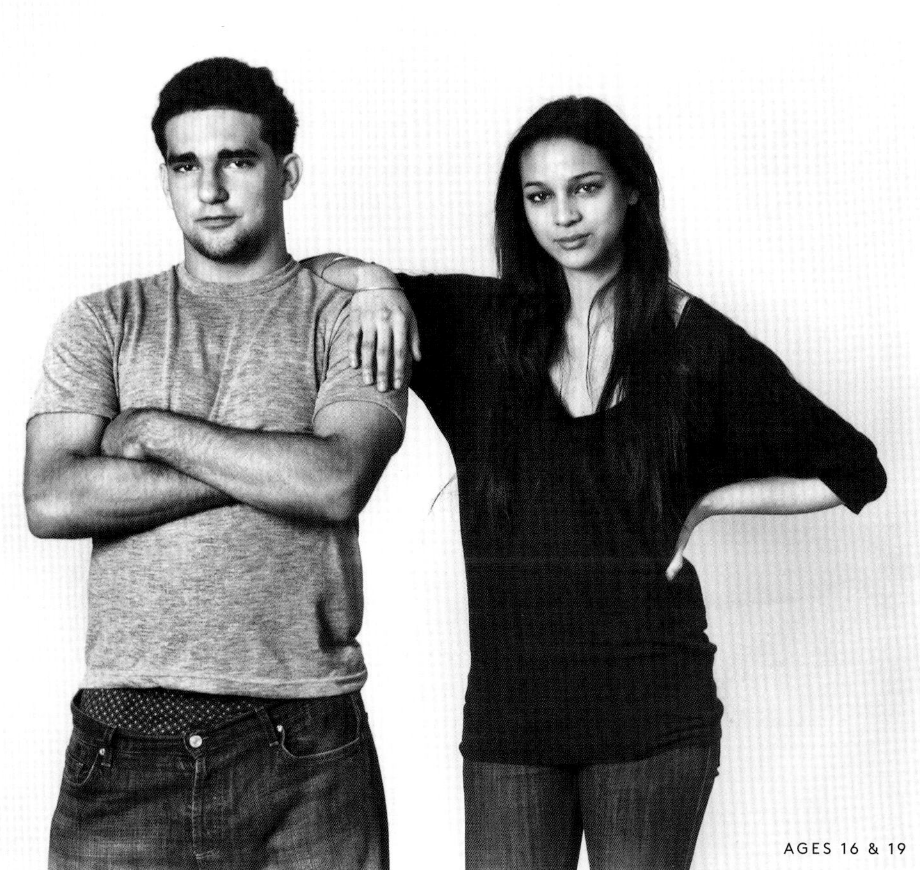

AGES 16 & 19

THEIR MOTHER: When I look at these pictures I think of all the expectations and hopes and dreams we have when they're babies. And, then, what ups and downs you go through in life. Then, they're gone. I love the last picture. They're such stunning people.

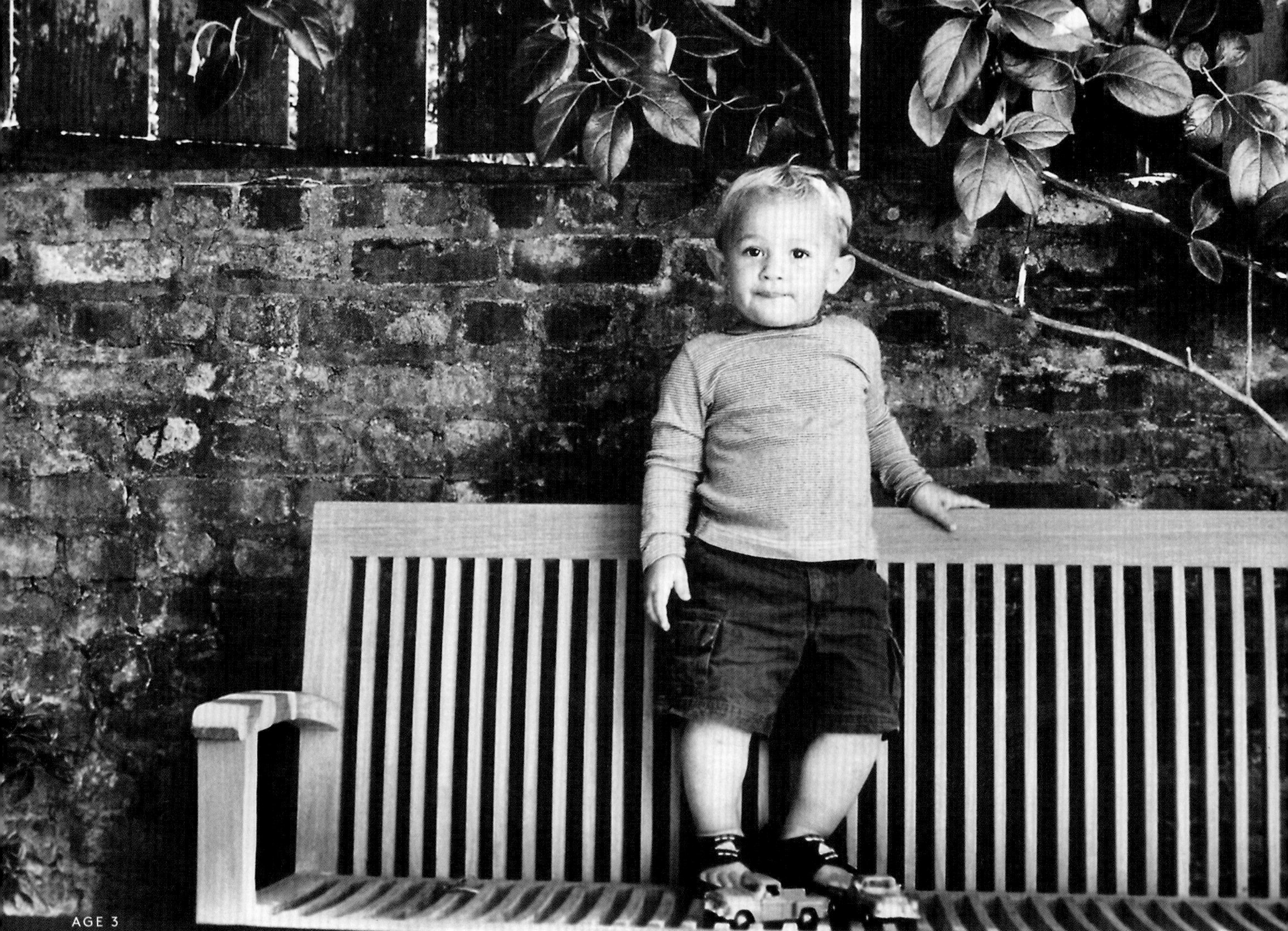
AGE 3

BENJAMIN, AT 12: I'm still curious and still like to annoy my sisters. The hardest thing about childhood is having your parents say "no" when you really want to do something. Like, "Can we stay one more minute?" Maybe something's going to happen but you have to go right before. I won't let my kid do everything he wants to — like play on the computer too much or have too much sugar. But I'd let them have electronics on weekends after they've done their homework. My parents won't let me do that anymore. Maybe they took it away because I was rushing homework. I think childhood ends when you go into high school. Some people say that childhood doesn't end until you leave home. But that's probably parents.

BENJAMIN

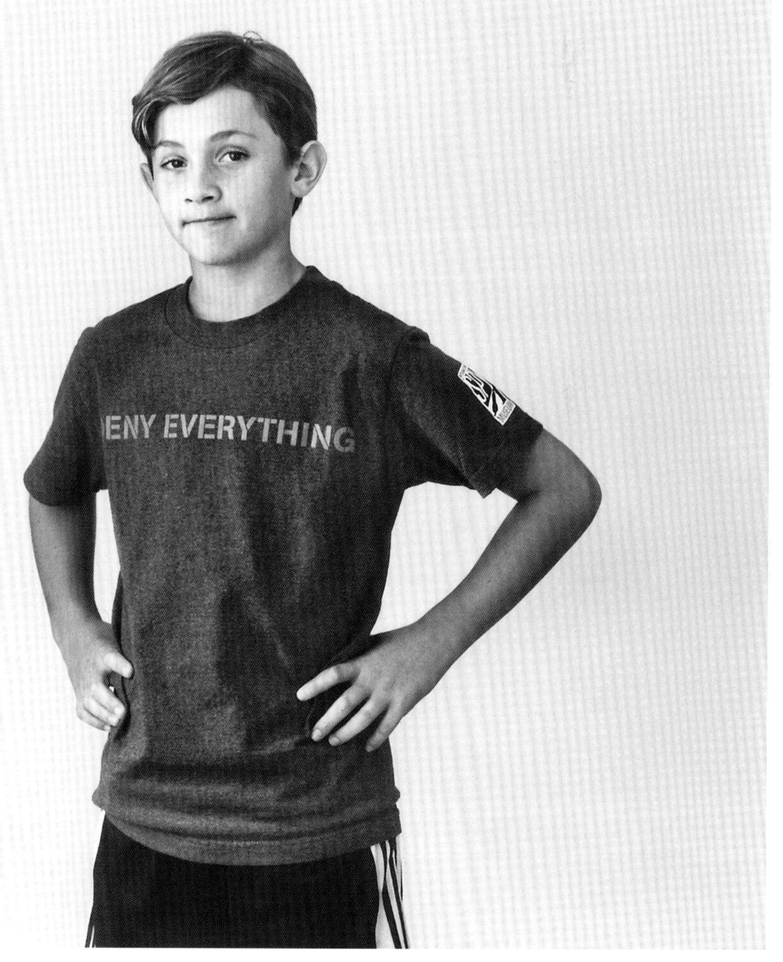

AGE 12

MARISA

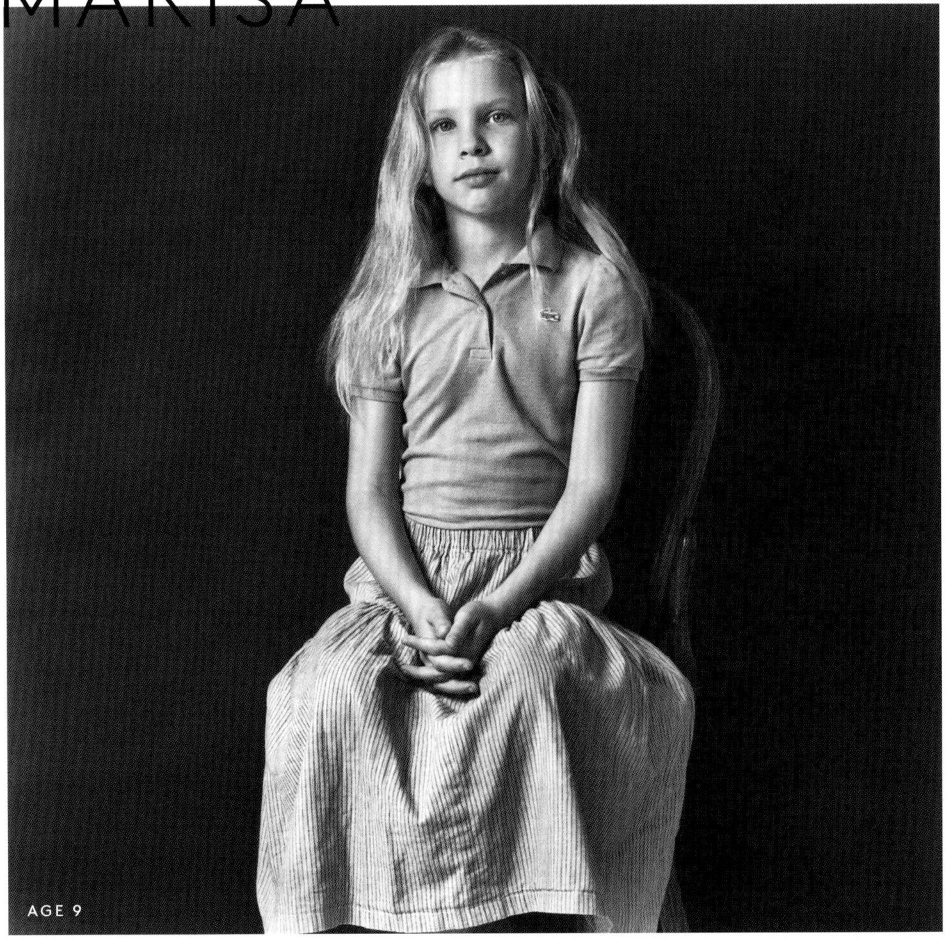

AGE 9

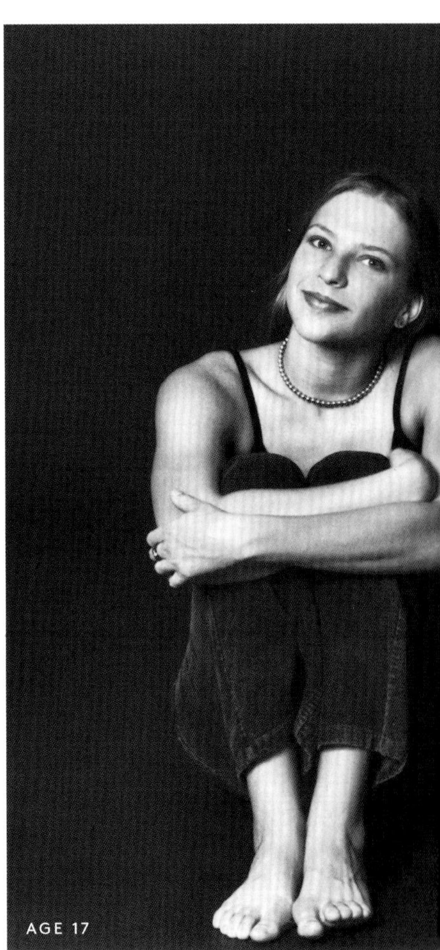

AGE 17

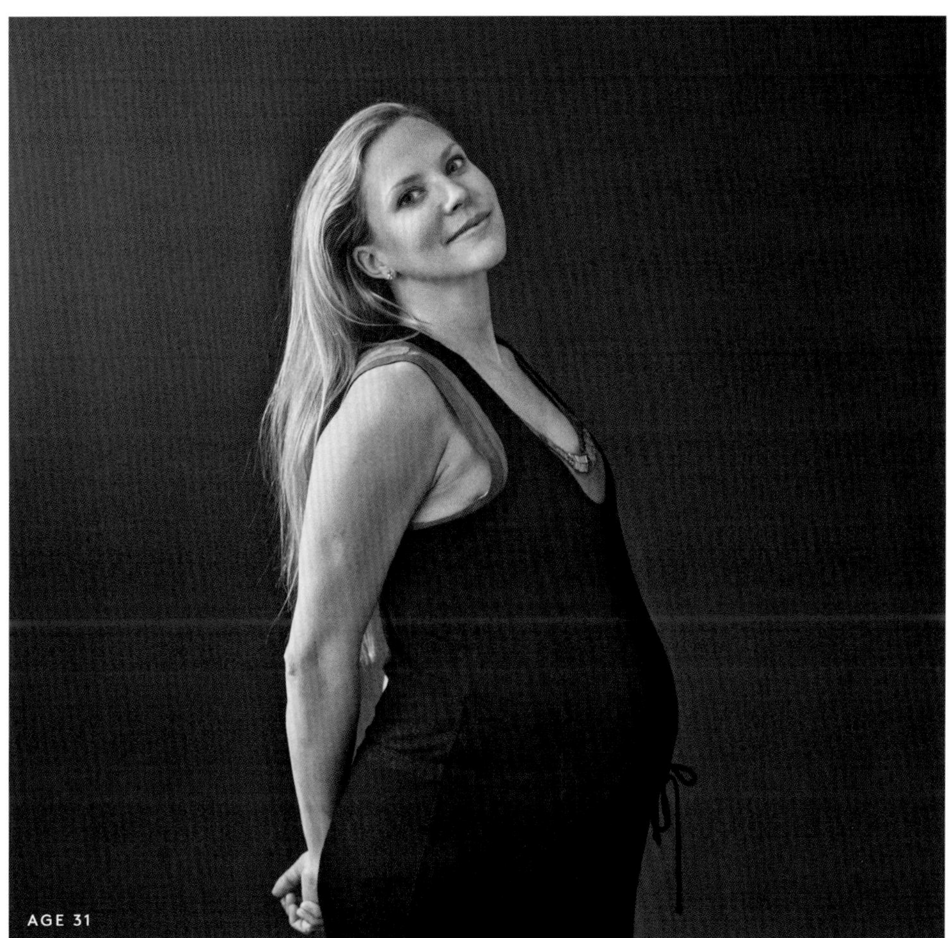

MARISA, AT 31: I'm the oldest of six children. People always ask me what it was like being in such a big family. That's almost always their first question to me. I say it was fun. I'm a young soul. Everything is always new to me. I'm happy.

MOE, ALEX & EMILY

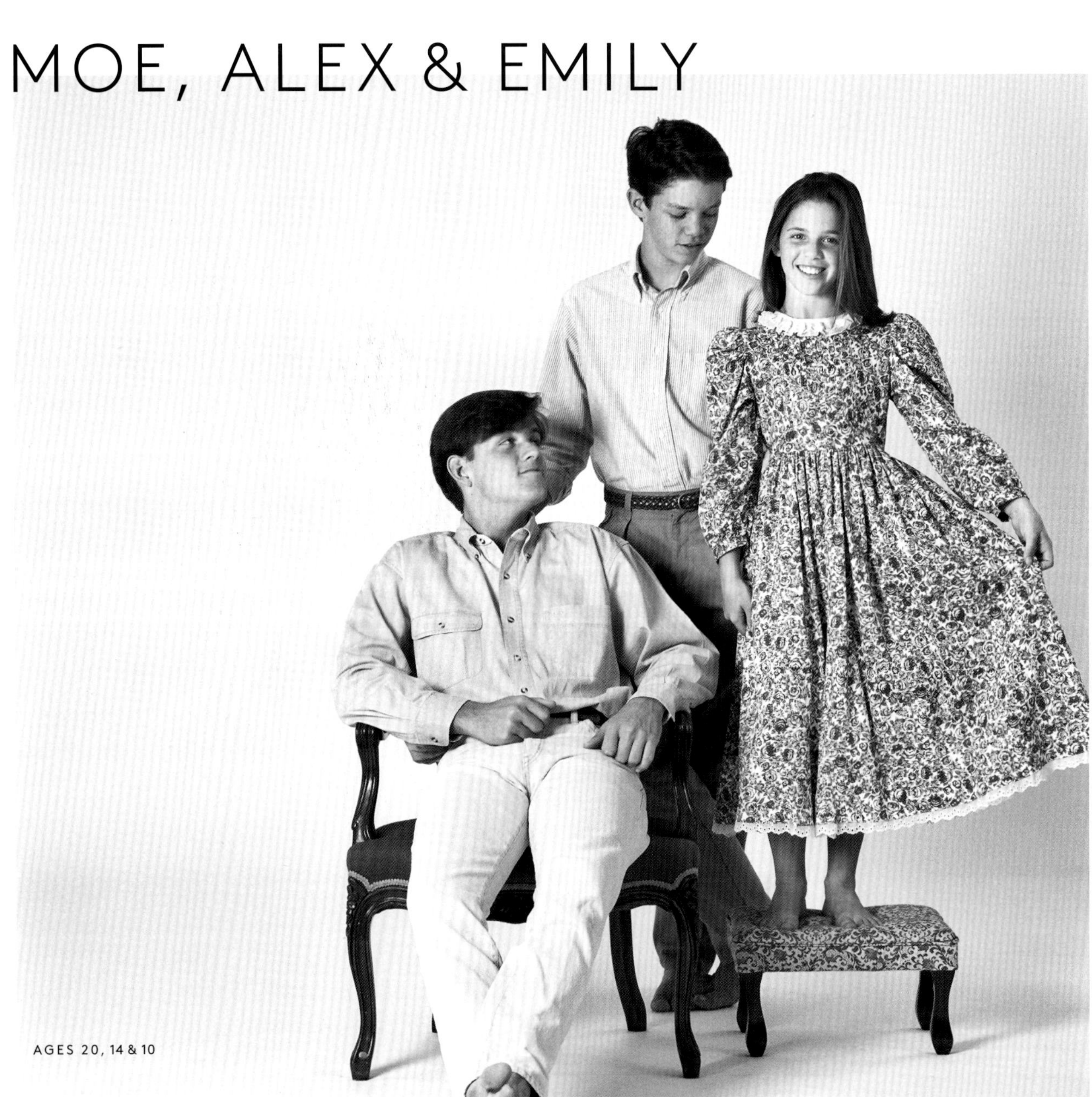

AGES 20, 14 & 10

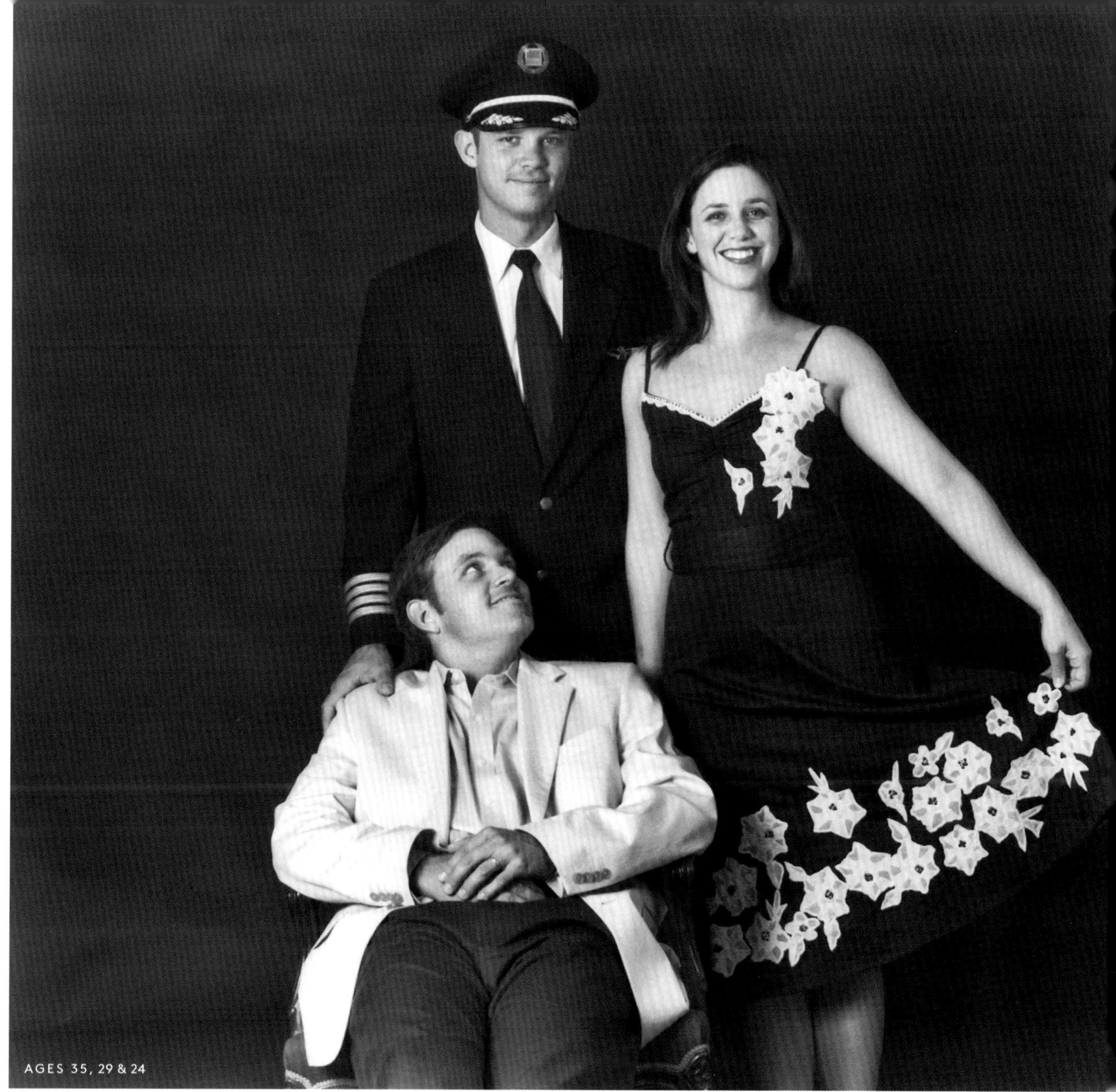
AGES 35, 29 & 24

THEIR MOTHER: I wanted my children to be independent, confident, and kind. And they are. I think it is a lot of luck. Also, good genes, safe environment, happy home, dinner together. I think we are closer now that we are all adults. People think we are weird because we like to meet places and have vacations together. The Lassie family we are called.

VICTORIA

AT 19: I remember first grade. I thought I was the smartest one. I was always super bossy. I'm sure I was telling people what to do during the Communion rehearsals. I have no shame in telling people if they're doing something wrong. I was the rebellious child. If my parents had let me learn from my own mistakes, that would have been better. And still, I always want to come home and be taken care of. I call my mom every day. Sometimes she just has to hang up; she's busy with something. I never want to have kids. I love other people's kids but I couldn't pay my own kids enough attention. A perfect day for me is to wake up from twelve hours of sleep. It's 75 degrees out and I go to the beach all day and then enjoy some really good tacos. It's really very simple.

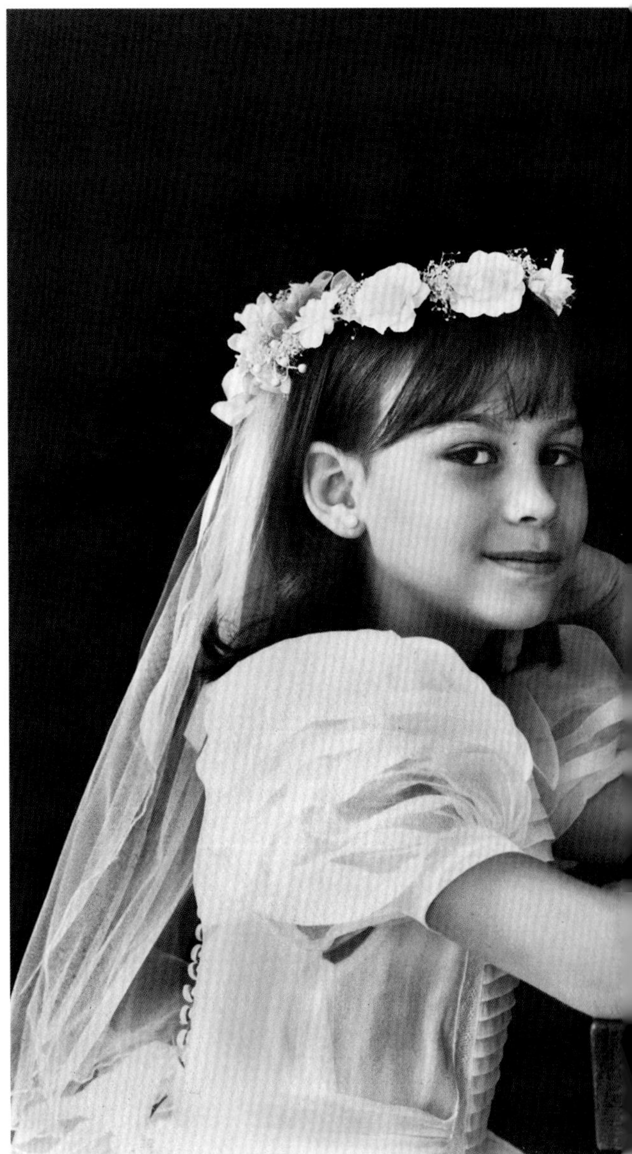

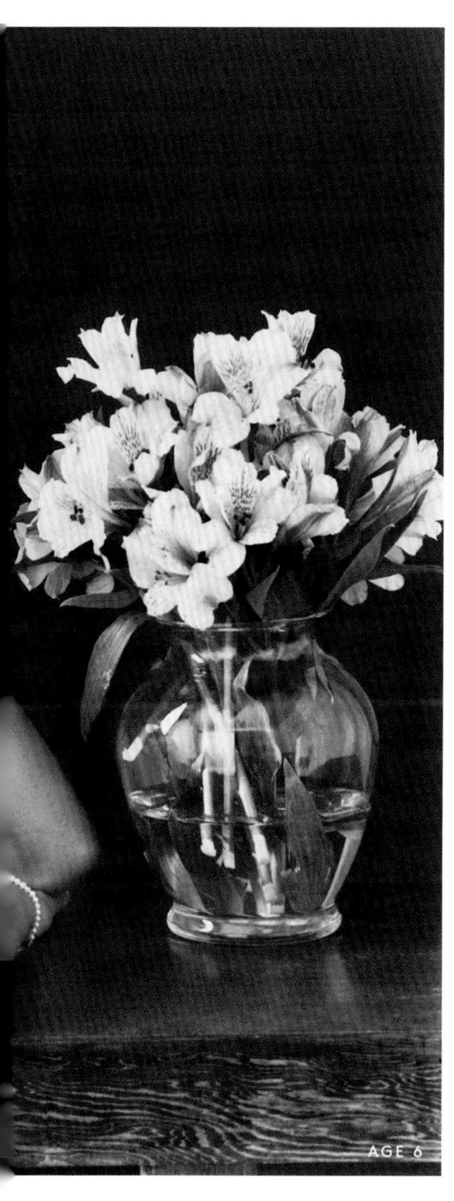
AGE 6

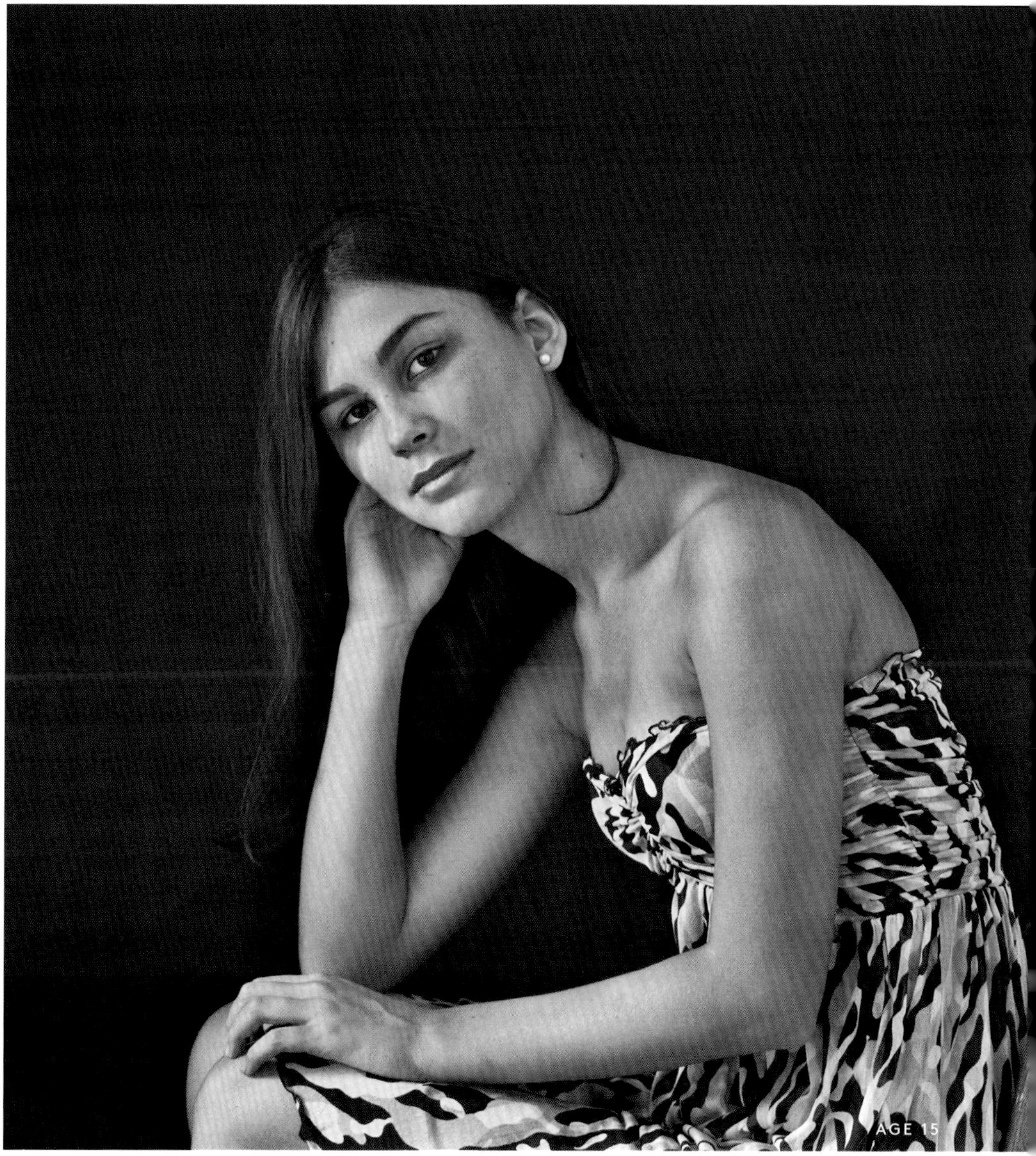

AGE 15

SOPHIE & GEORGIA

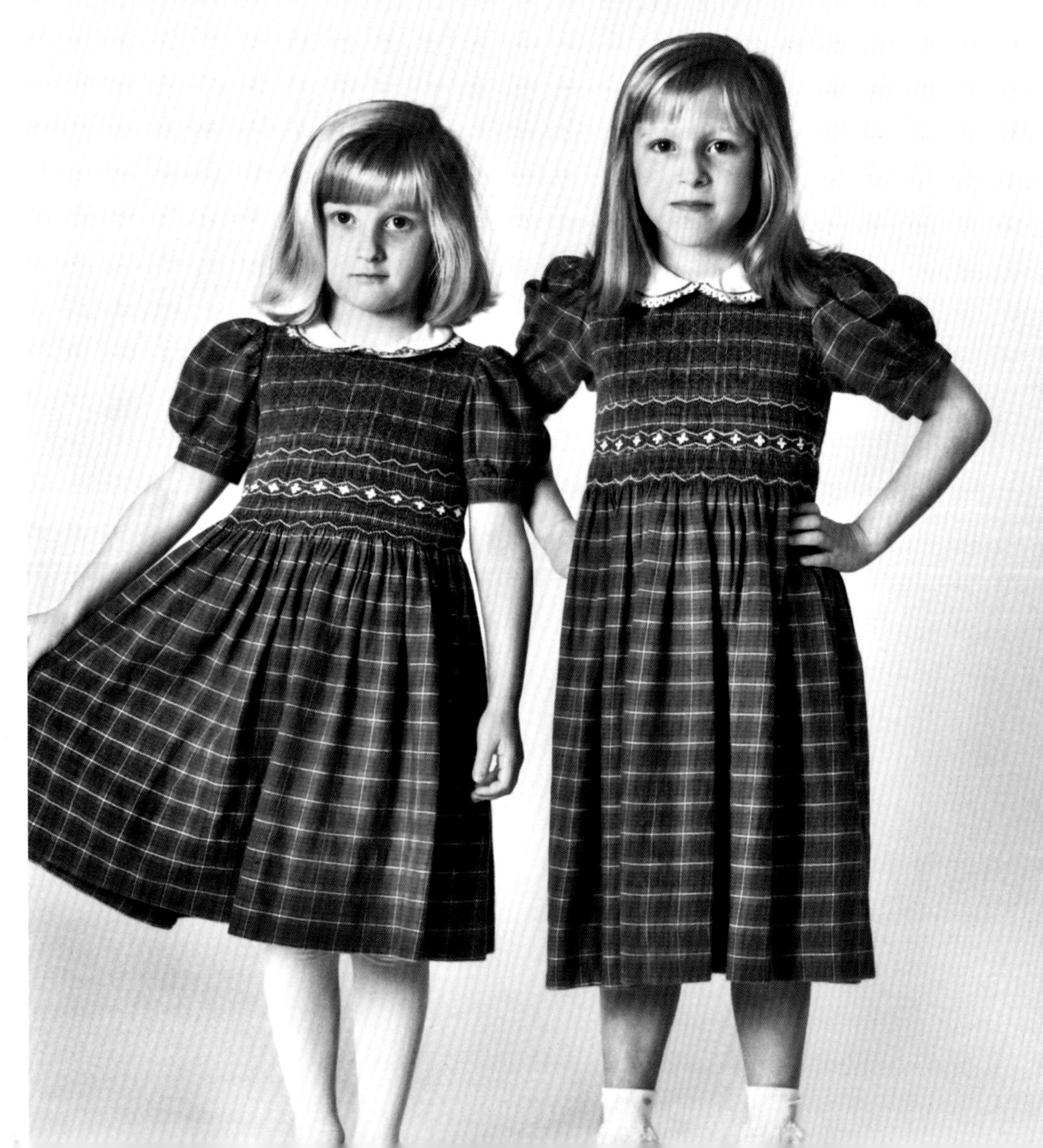

AGES 6 & 7

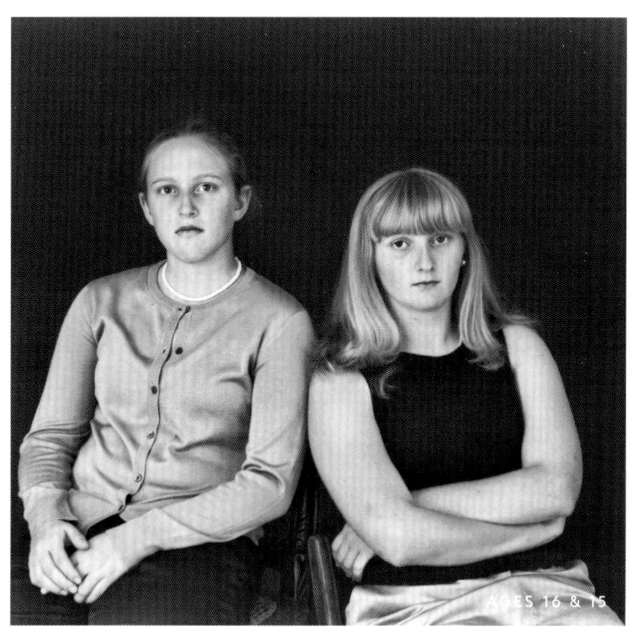

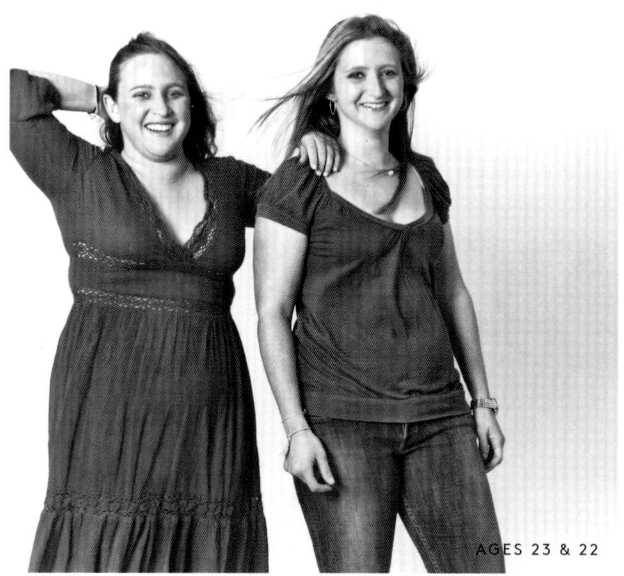

GEORGIA, AT 26: I didn't like wearing dresses. I would scream and cry when I had to. SOPHIE, AT 24: In the second photo, I look pissed off. GEORGIA: I kept to myself a lot. I don't think I look approachable. SOPHIE: No, I think you were bored. SOPHIE: I'm highly attached to Georgia. GEORGIA: She's like a puppy. GEORGIA: I'm a thinking person, sometimes too much. But now I can turn it off. When I was seven, I did what seven-year-olds shouldn't be doing: I thought all the time. SOPHIE: I still like to dress up and be the center of attention; I require constant attention. When I was little, I thought I'd be powerful. I wanted people to know me. GEORGIA: When I was little I couldn't imagine being away from my parents. I couldn't even spend the night at my grandparents. I was afraid that something would go wrong at home if I weren't there. I always thought "what if." At least I'd be there. SOPHIE: I was desperate not to be a little girl. GEORGIA: I couldn't make sense out of it. It wasn't pleasant. When you're young you think that no one could ever understand what you're about.

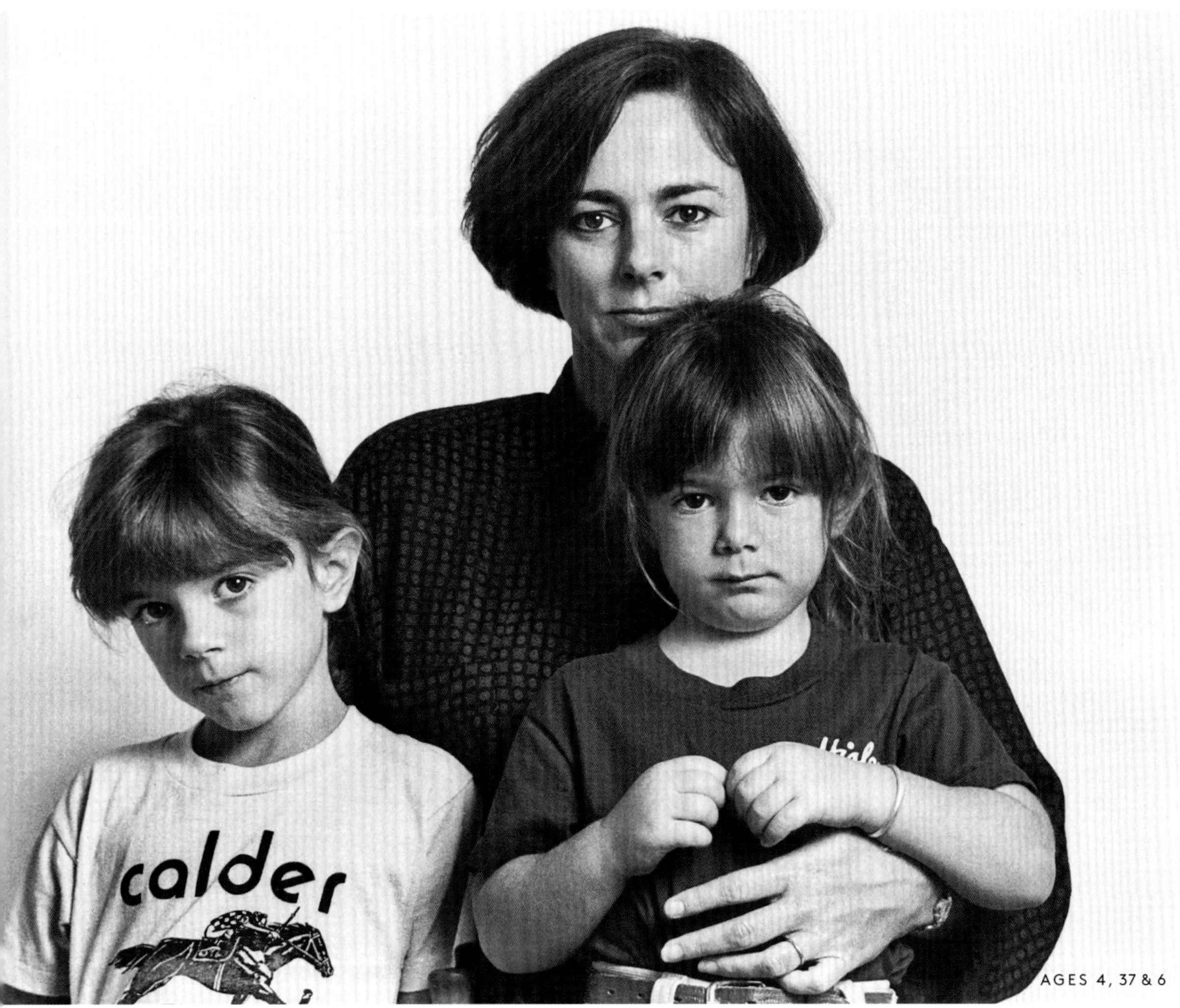

AGES 4, 37 & 6

LOUISE, AT 61: When I look at the first picture, I'm thirty-seven again. I have the second photo in a guest room. Once a guest told me he loved the picture because, he said, "You're like a tigress: I will put your eyes out and kill you if you even think twice about coming near these two." I thought the best part about raising children was watching the unfolding. I didn't need to know their future. When our second child was born, my husband decided to work from home. He didn't want to miss anything. We did everything as a four-person unit. He never missed a play or their horse shows. The kids thought he didn't work. **SARAH, AT 27:** In class when they asked what your parents do, I said Mom colored. **AUBREY, AT 30:** Some other kids said their dad was an attorney so I said mine was, too. He's a horse trainer; he'd rather die than be an attorney. **LOUISE:** One night I go out at midnight with a bucket and a flashlight to pick snails off the plants. I see a leg coming out my daughter's window. **AUBREY:** It wasn't me; it was my friend. My mom said just one line: "It's a bit much." Once when I was coming home at 8:00 a.m. and my mom was coming out, I think that's what she said again: "It's a bit much." I agreed. **LOUISE:** They weren't angels. **AUBREY:** We loved you so much. I always left you a note. Then if I didn't come home, at least there would be a note. **LOUISE:** I never saw a note. **AUBREY:** Because you didn't go in my room, looking for me. I knew if you came in and we weren't there it would be the worst thing ever. I left my diary out, too. I knew you would never read it. You respected our privacy. Now that I have children, I'm putting bars on their windows.

SARAH, LOUISE & AUBREY

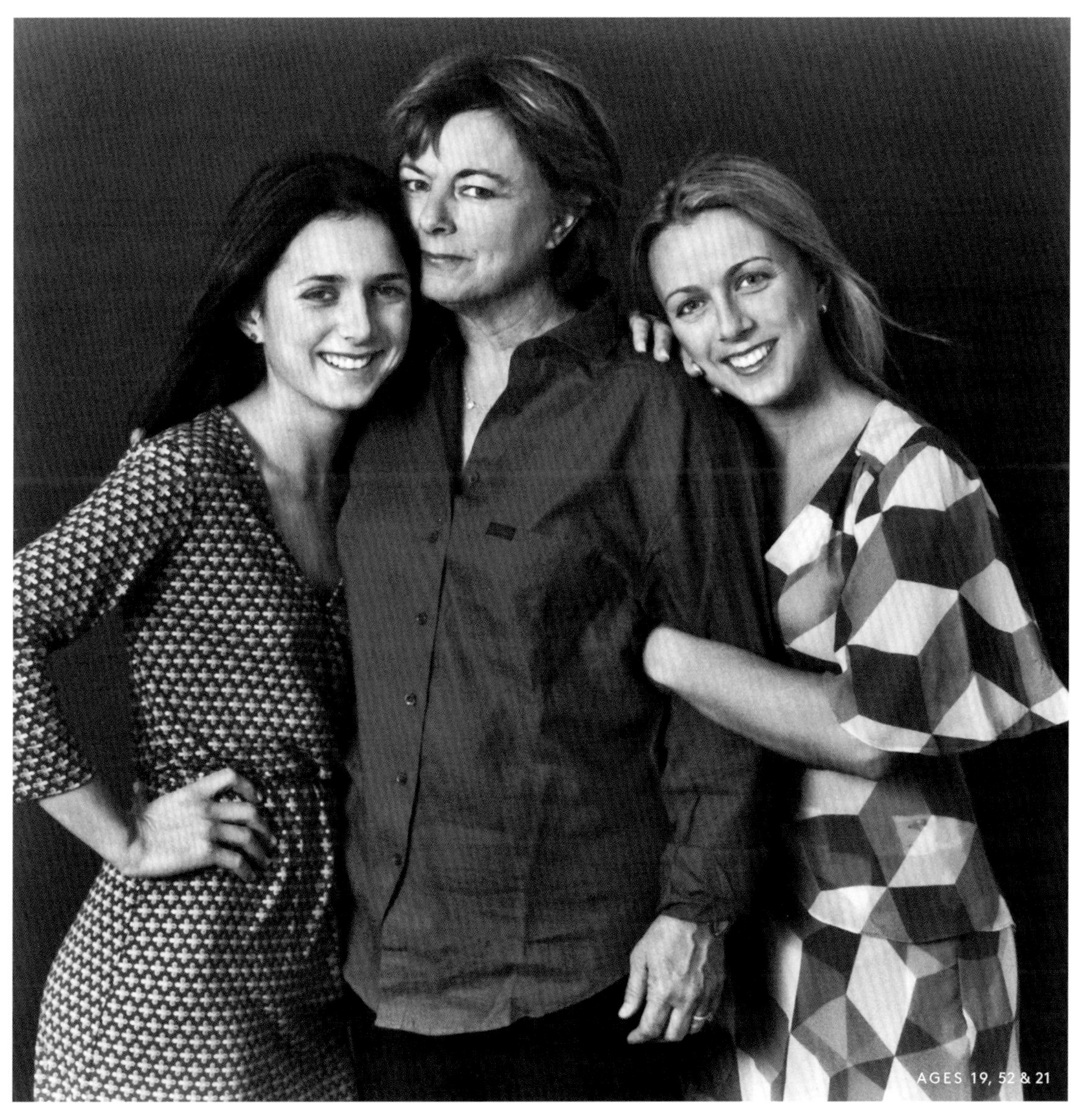

AGES 19, 52 & 21

GABRIEL & HAROLD

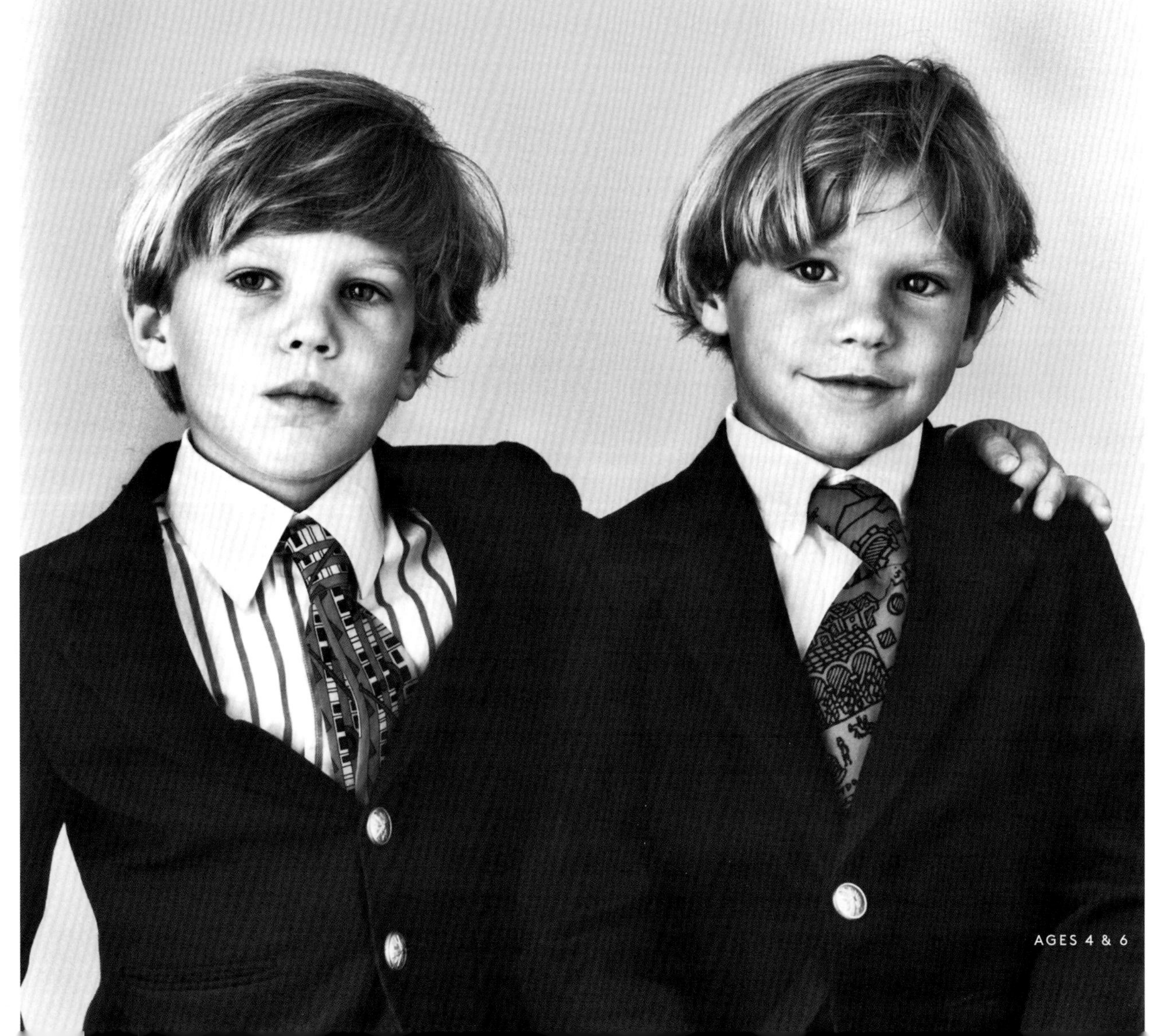

AGES 4 & 6

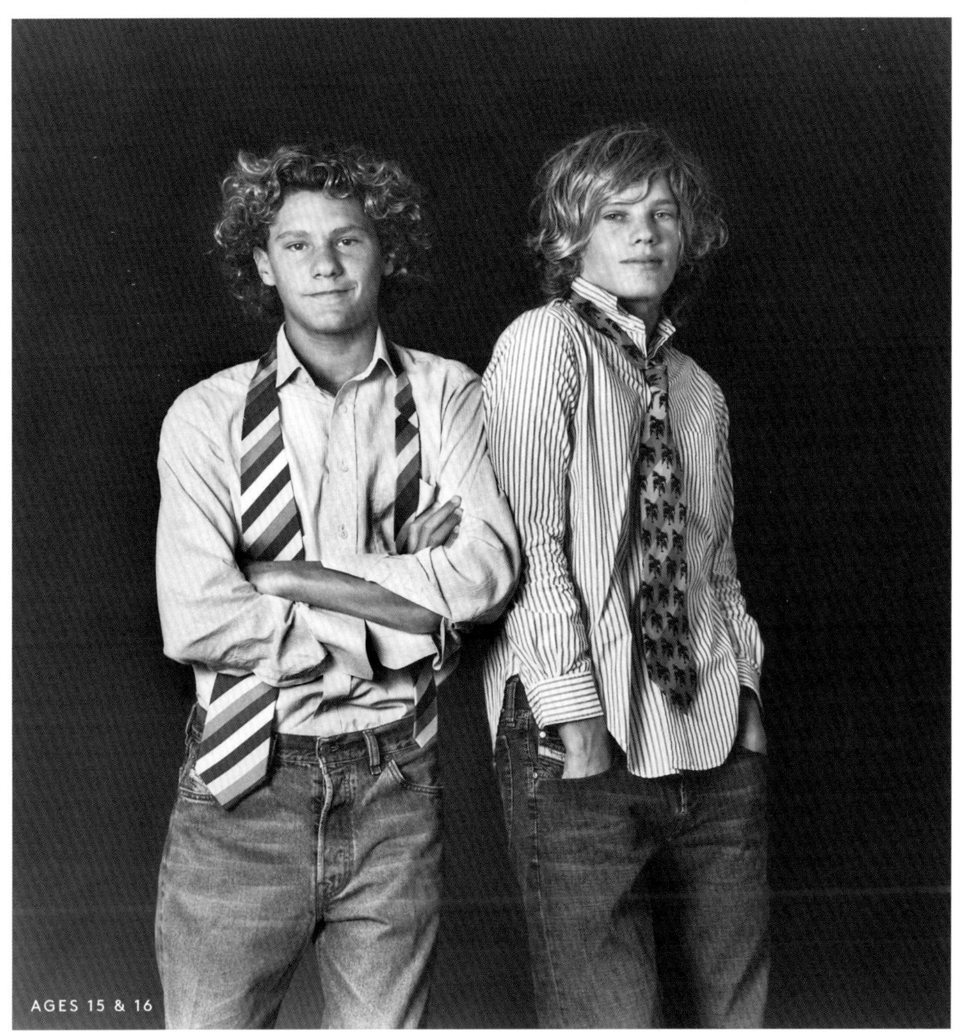

HAROLD, AT 19: Is childhood slow? In one sense, I'm still in my childhood. **GABE, AT 20:** When you're super young, it goes fast.

COLIN

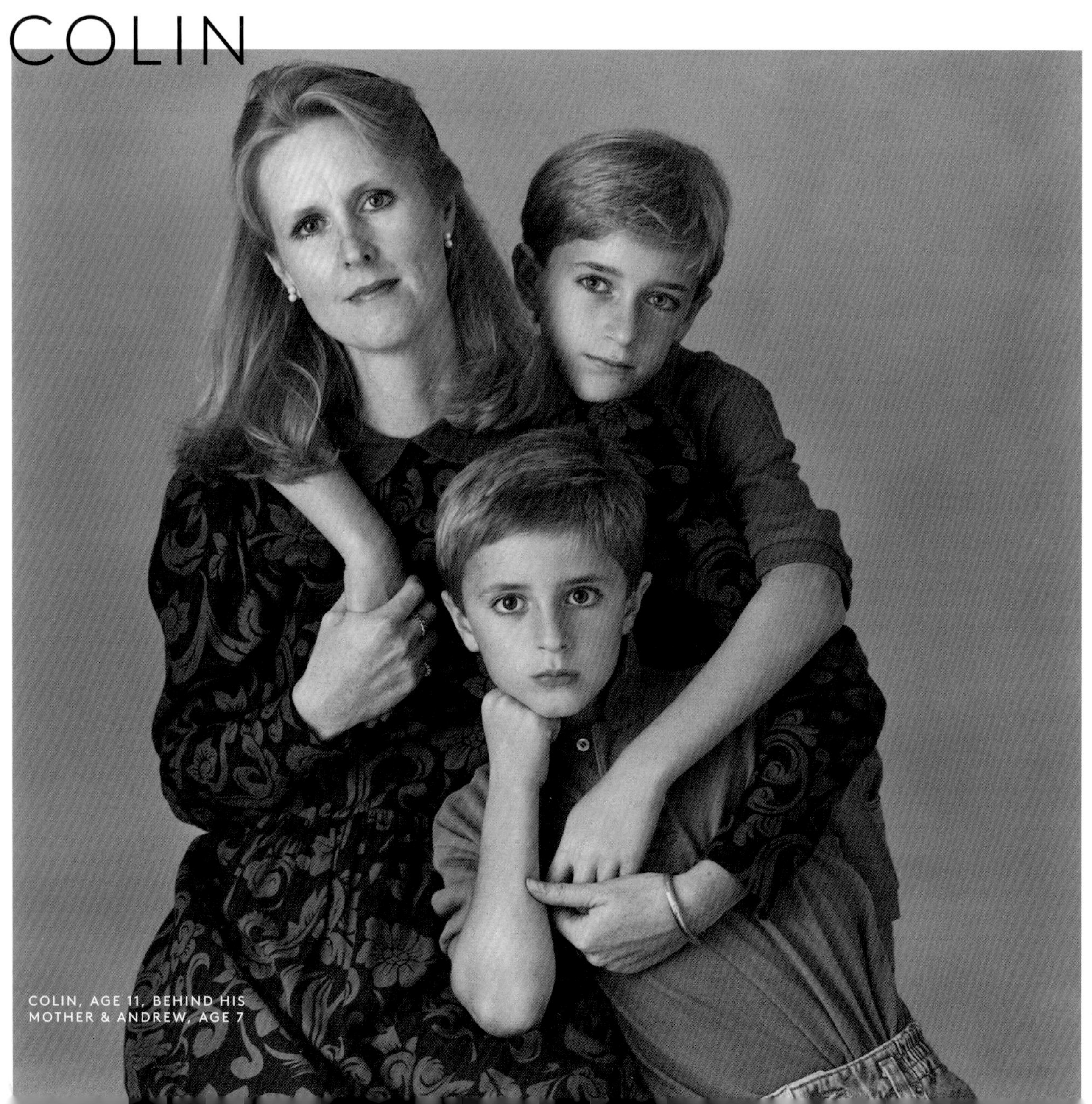

COLIN, AGE 11, BEHIND HIS MOTHER & ANDREW, AGE 7

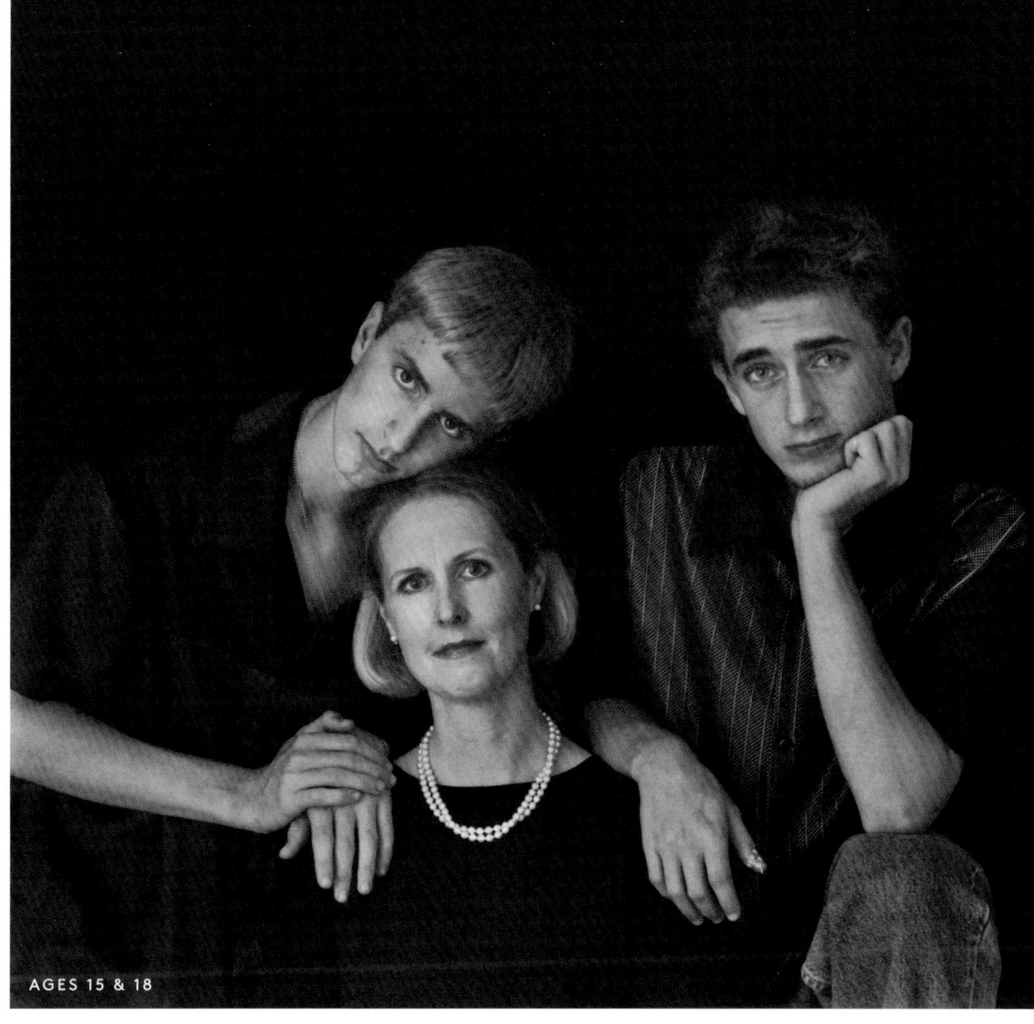

AGES 15 & 18

COLIN, AT 30: Looking at this first picture reminds me of how shy and insecure I was. Almost like I'm hiding behind my mum and brother. In the second picture I'm trying to convince myself that I'm cool. I was at the pinnacle of my insecurity at that time in my life. I really had no idea who I was or what I liked. I was trying to get away from being the kid who had the haircut his mom picked and wore the shirt his mom chose. My brother and I had developed an adult friendship by the time of the second pictures. He is probably my most favorite person on the planet. I find it really interesting to look at myself here, perhaps seeming confident, but really simply having become fairly good at covering up the rough spots. It makes me really happy and grateful to be where I am today, in a much more genuinely confident place. I've been a hopeless romantic since I was six. Children are mean, everyone knows that. What kids don't know is that none of it means anything. At least I didn't. I wish I could have seen some of the teasing and jostling for popularity as I see it now. It might have made life smoother. I still want certain things for my life, but I'm pretty happy with how things are now. I would say to parents, be consistently emotionally available for your children. My parents have done a fabulous job. Don't be afraid to let your children make mistakes.

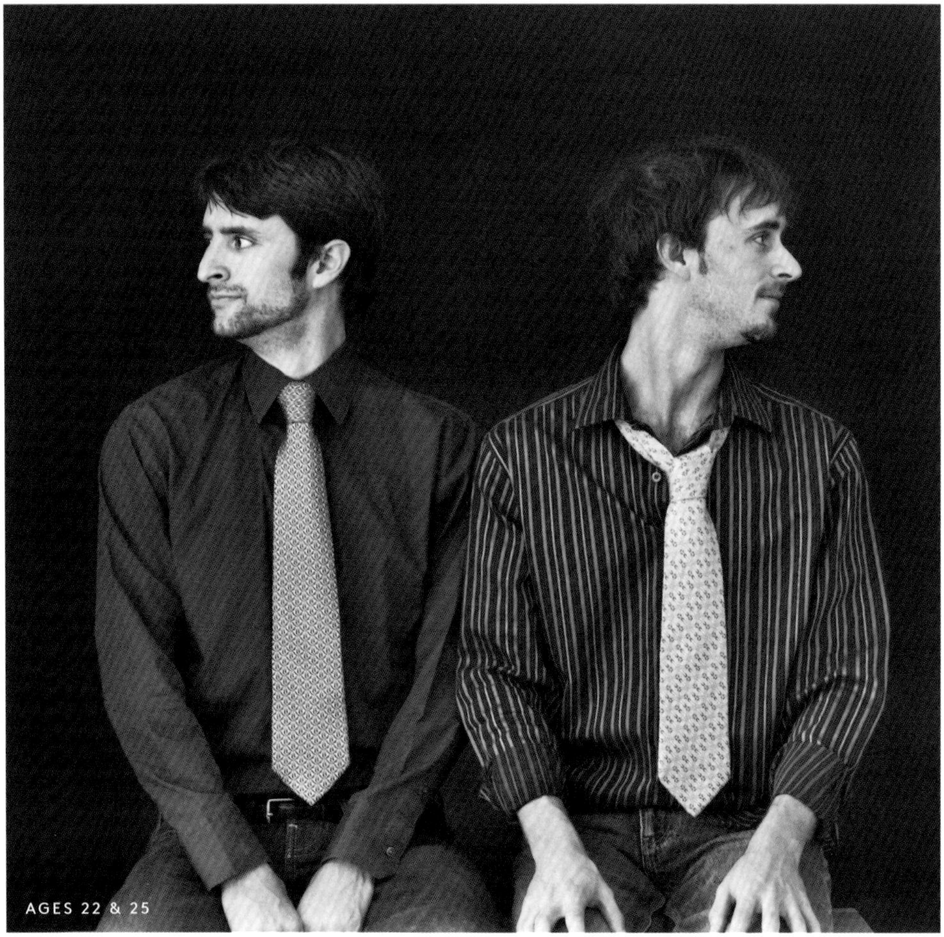

AGES 22 & 25

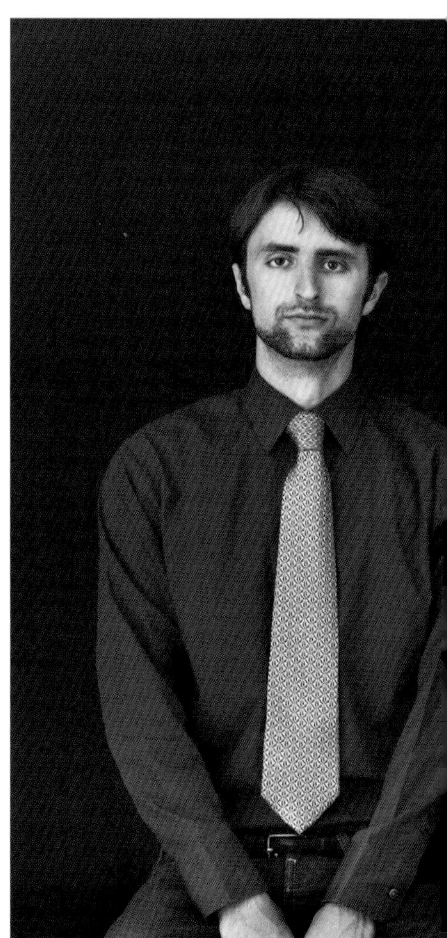

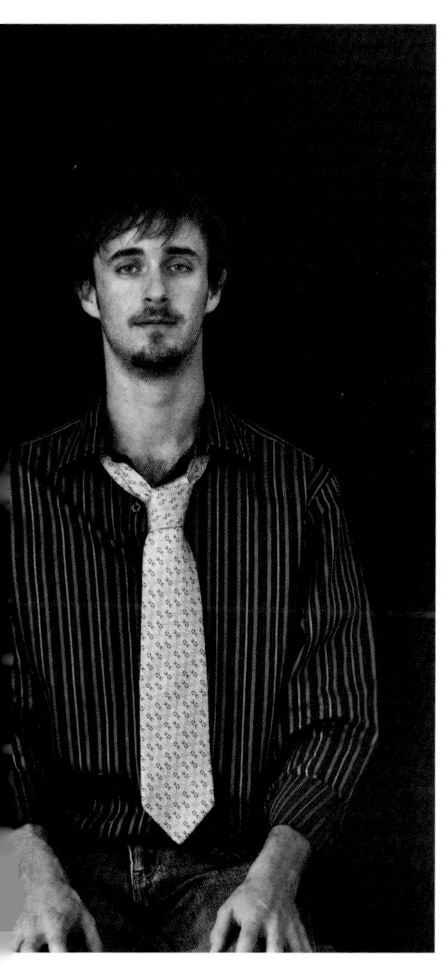

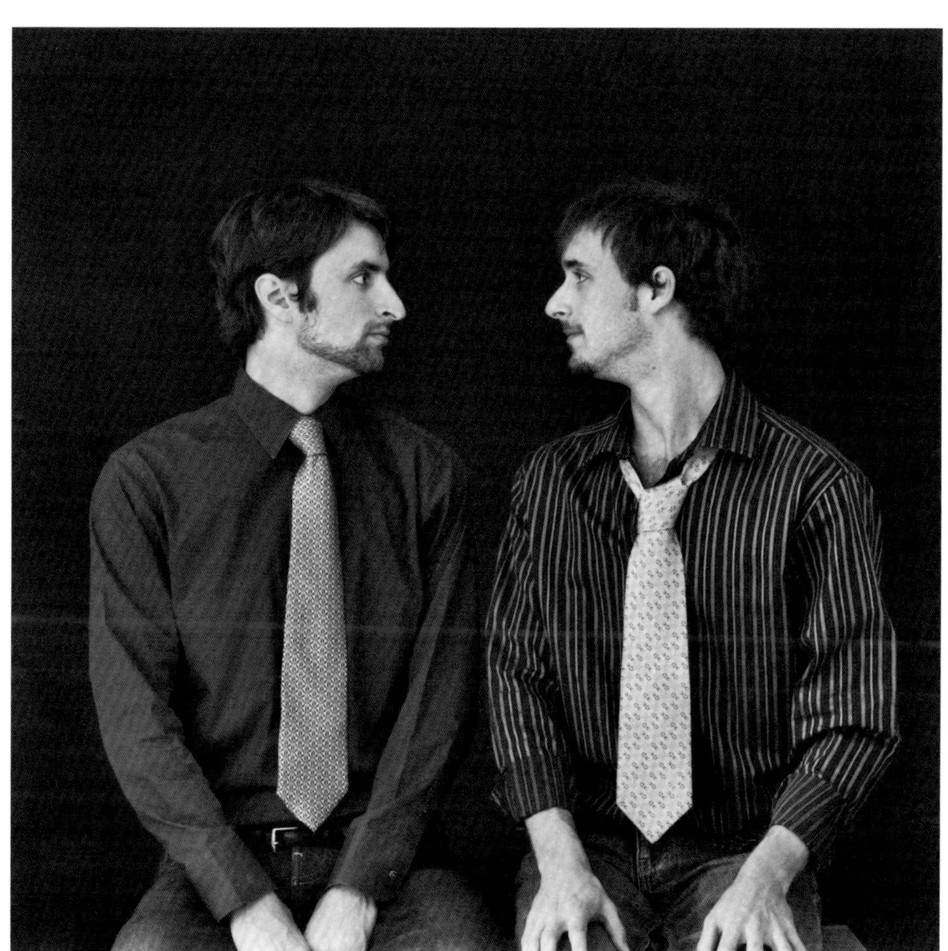

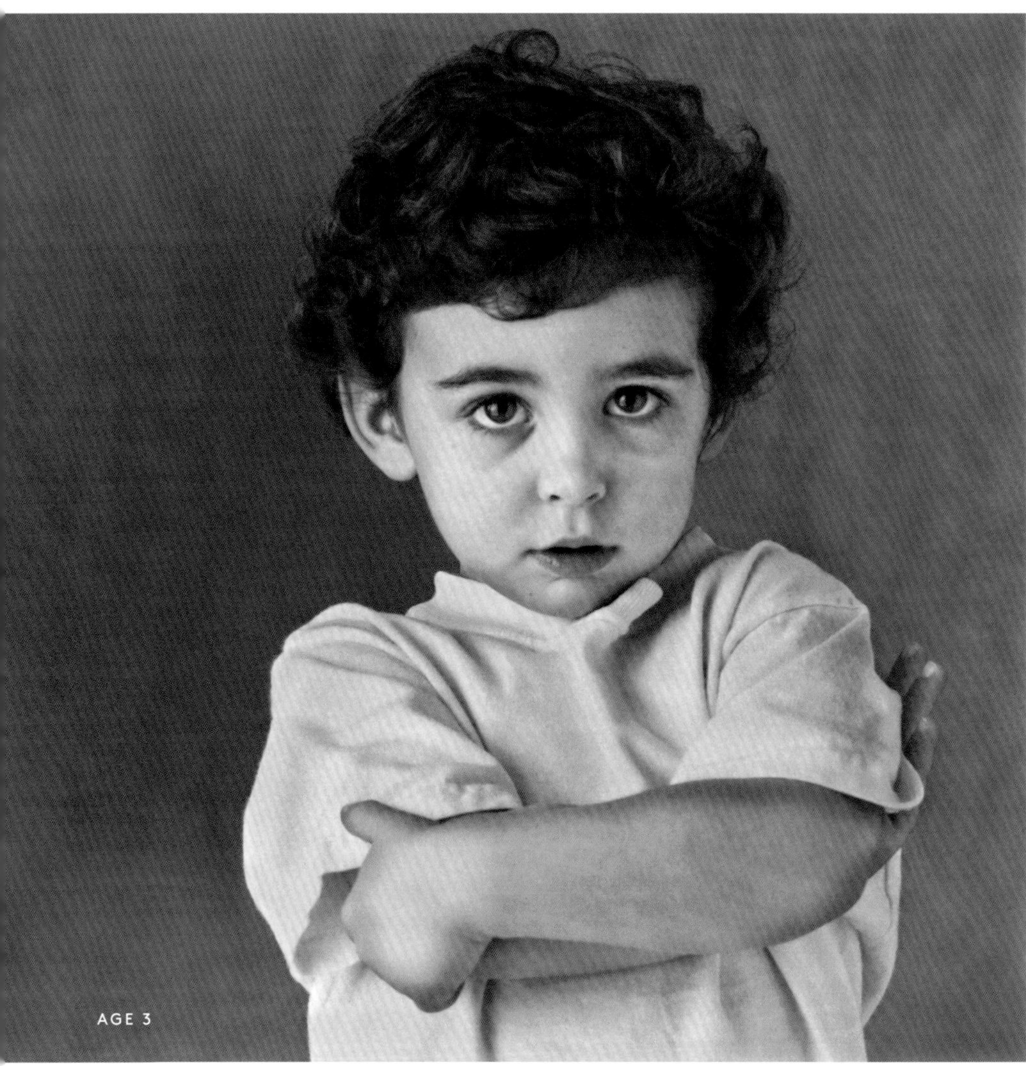

JONAH, AT 20: The first photograph is the best example of what I am. As you go further back, it represents you more. The older you get the more conscious you are of yourself. When you're younger you don't remember thinking outside yourself. I like things you don't have to talk about.

JONAH

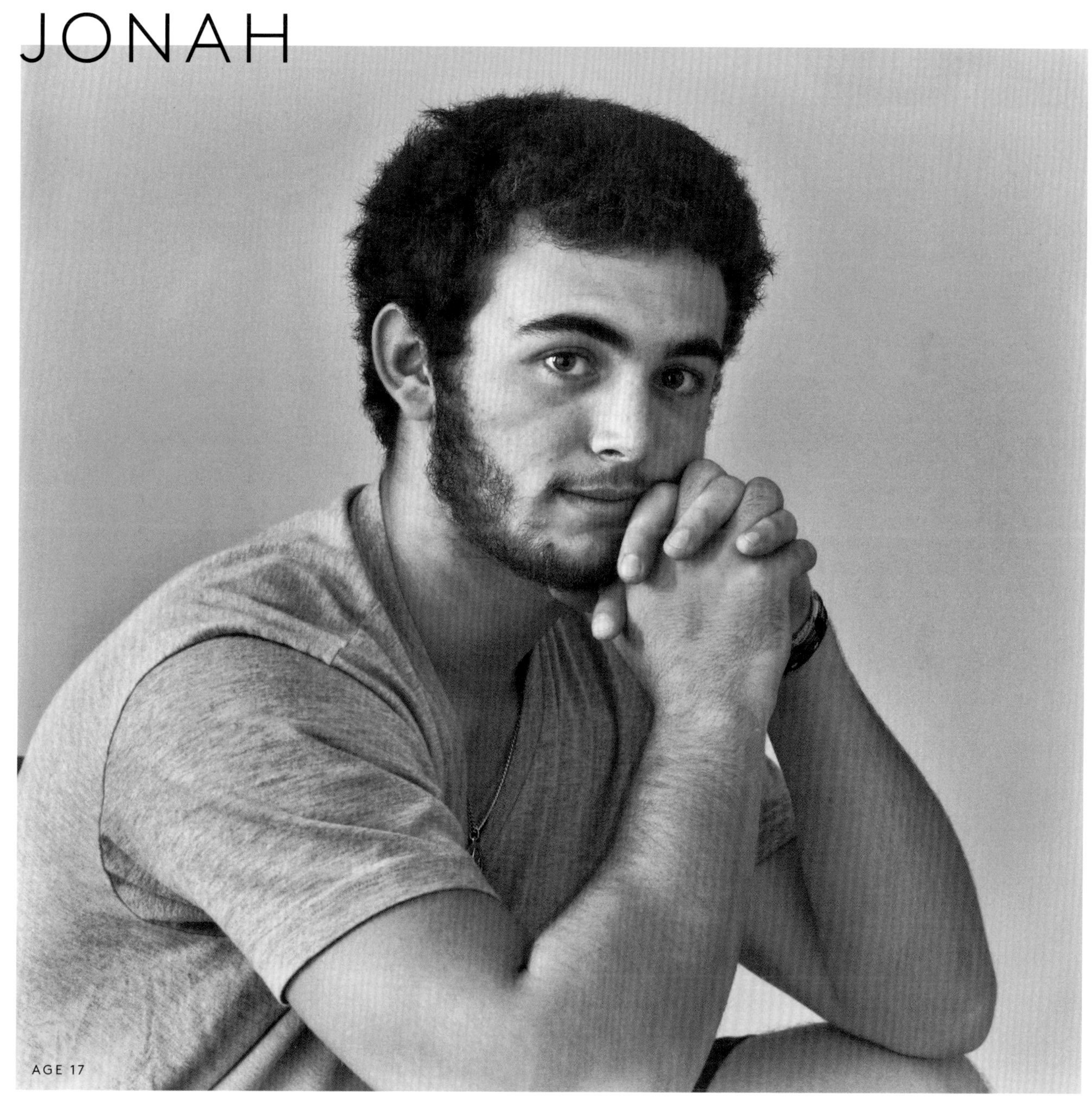

AGE 17

JULIA

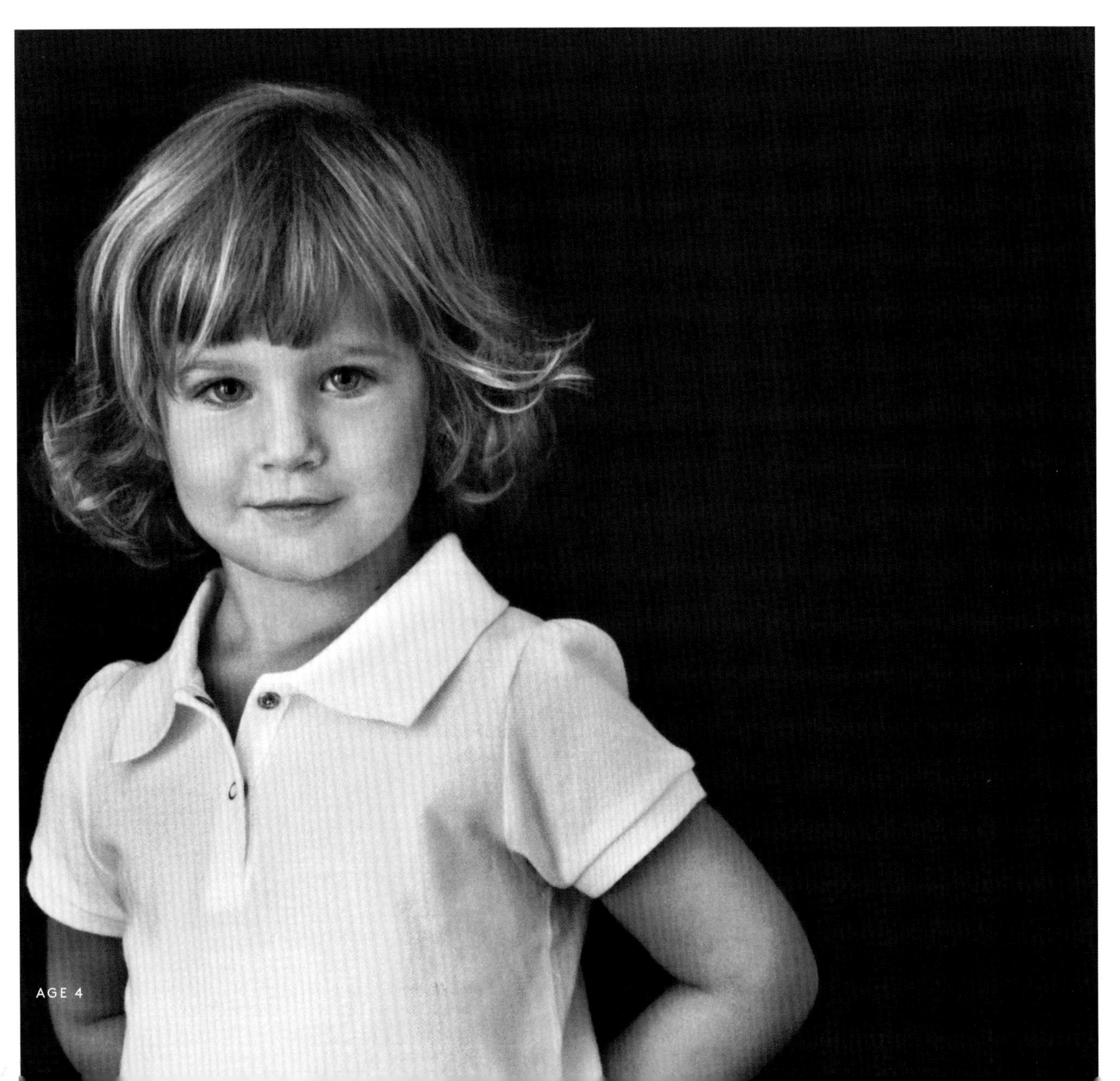
AGE 4

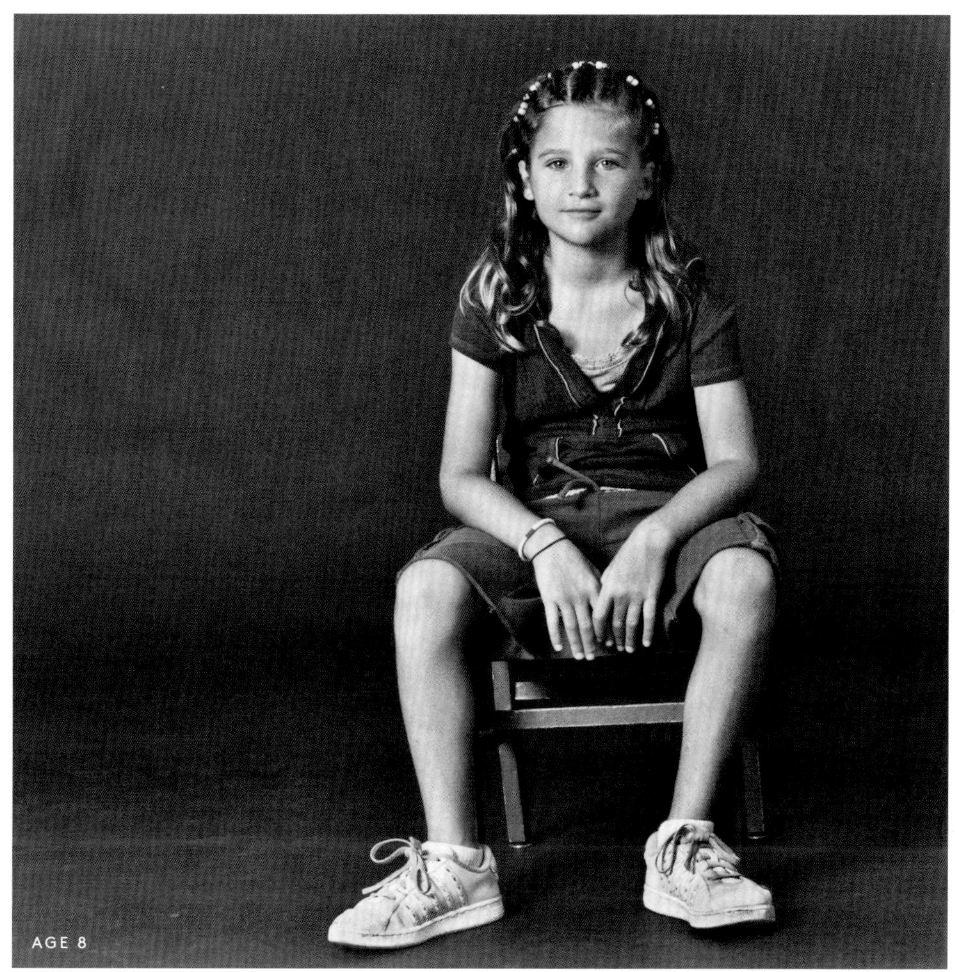
AGE 8

JULIA, AT 11: What's the same? My face, my organs, my soul. Souls don't change. Your soul is your heart, not your organ heart but when you love someone or don't like someone. I look more into the past than the future. I know the future is going to come and I can change it but my past is already there. I think about my memories, I look at my photo albums. Sometimes, time goes so fast: I'm in first period and then I'm in fifth period already.

ANNA & ARIELA

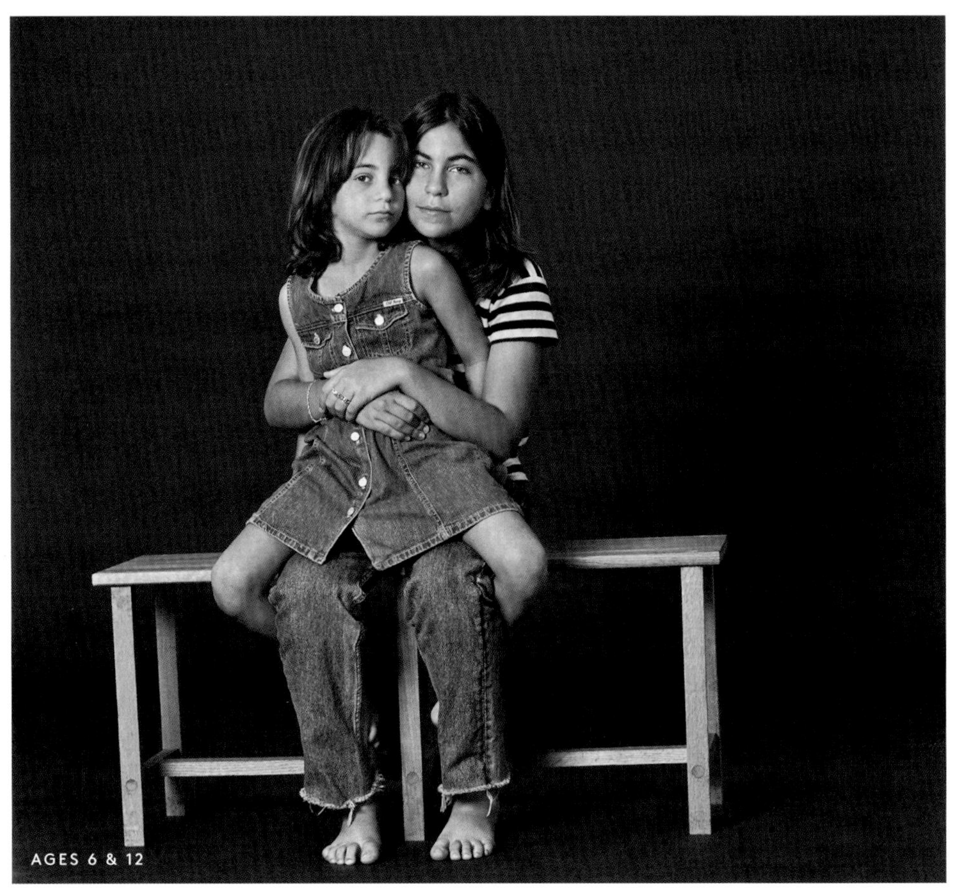

AGES 6 & 12

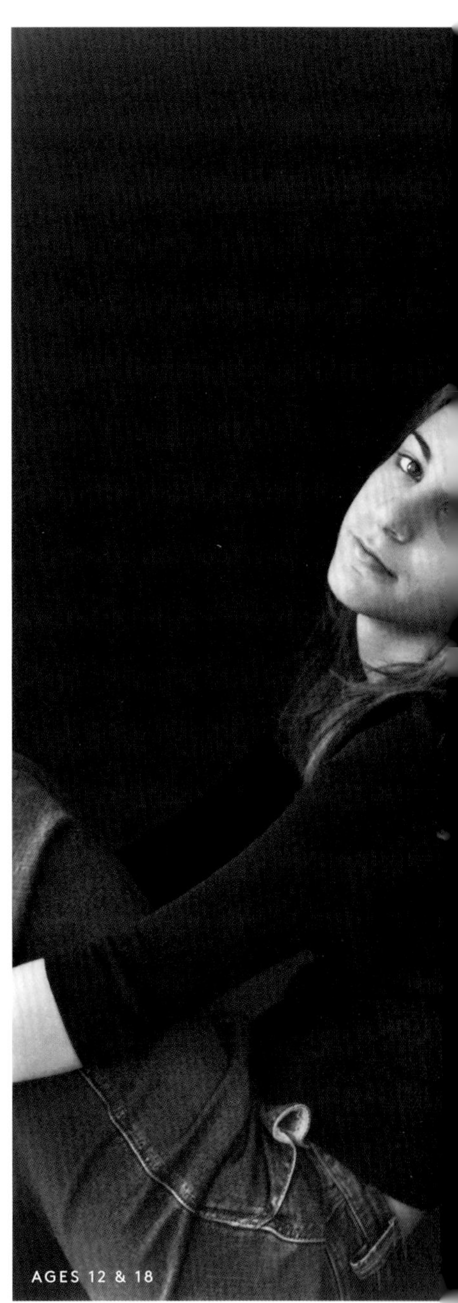

AGES 12 & 18

THEIR FATHER: I didn't think of them as intimate — there's a six-year difference in their ages. But when I look at the photos, they seem so close: I like to think that was really there. Still, I understand my limitations in understanding them. I knew time was going by so I tried to engage with them as much as I could. Now I'm a few years behind in how I think of them. Sometimes I treat them like they're still children. We talk every day. Sometimes there are several texts, snippets. We're always in touch. When I was growing up there was a stay-at-home mom and my hardworking dad. My father was present but distracted. I had a happy childhood but I didn't try to emulate it for my kids.

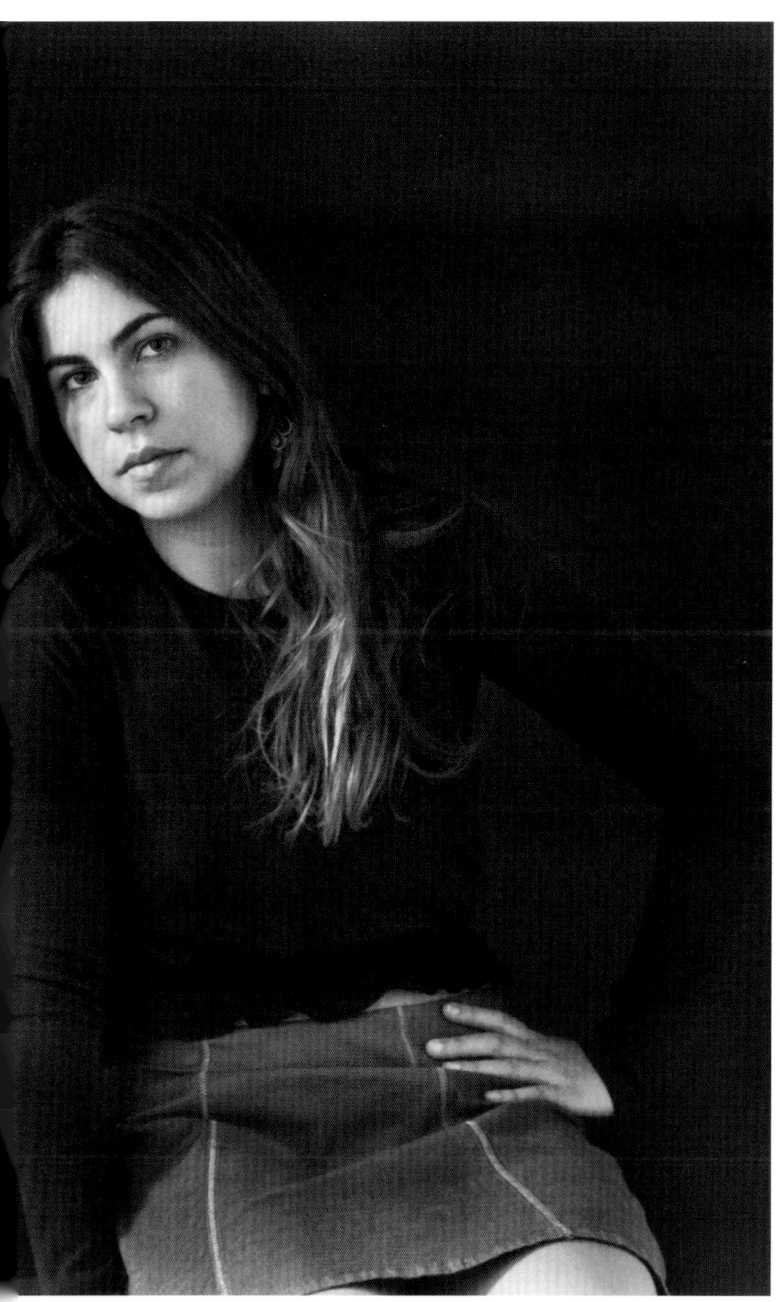

THEIR MOTHER: Their father was an over-equal parent. I could never read to them — he did. Children were an important choice for us. We had both gone to law school, worked, and were married fifteen years before deciding to have children. We never felt put upon, it was something we really wanted. We had already been out on Saturday night for eighteen years. They're way over the top of everything we think about or worry about. People say we'd be less anxious if they were settled. What does that mean?

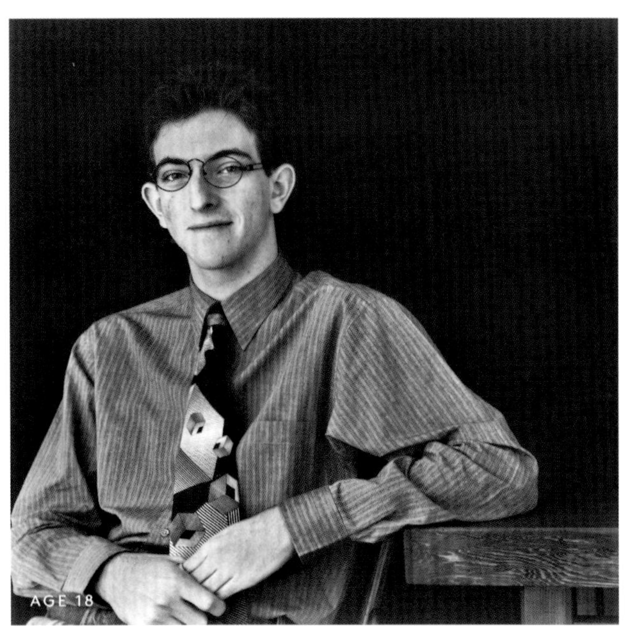
AGE 18

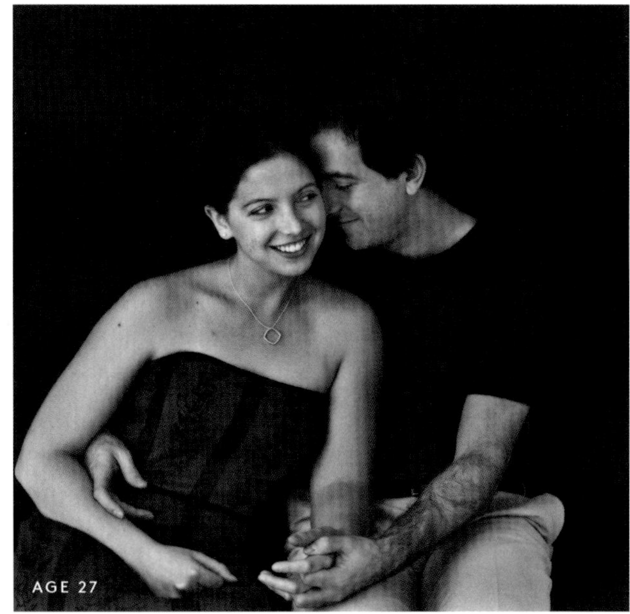
AGE 27

JUSTIN, AT 30: The first photo was during my senior year. I remember feeling like the king of the world. I was the yearbook editor and I was sure I was going to get into MIT. And I did, two weeks later. The second photo was taken right before Margaret and I got married. Margaret is wearing my favorite dress! She looks so beautiful! The third photo is just a couple of short years later. Who would have guessed I would have a child! It's really amazing how each photo was taken at a pivotal moment. I've known who I was since four years old. I just needed time to attain my goals — and I've completed all I can think of. Maybe it's time to think of new goals. I couldn't wait to get moving and start my own life. I was always independent and needed to get out of Miami — a city I never really liked.

JUSTIN

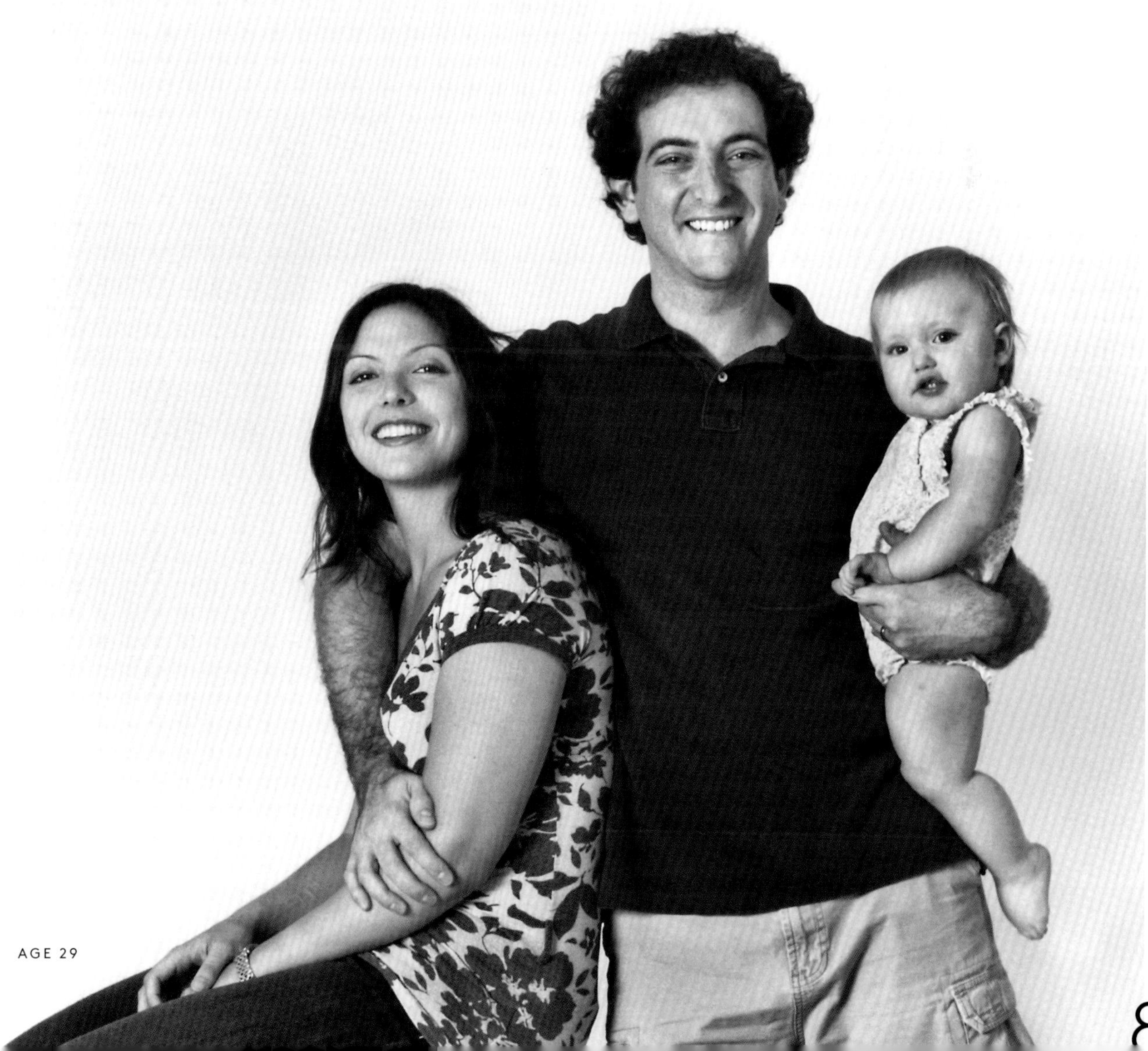

AGE 29

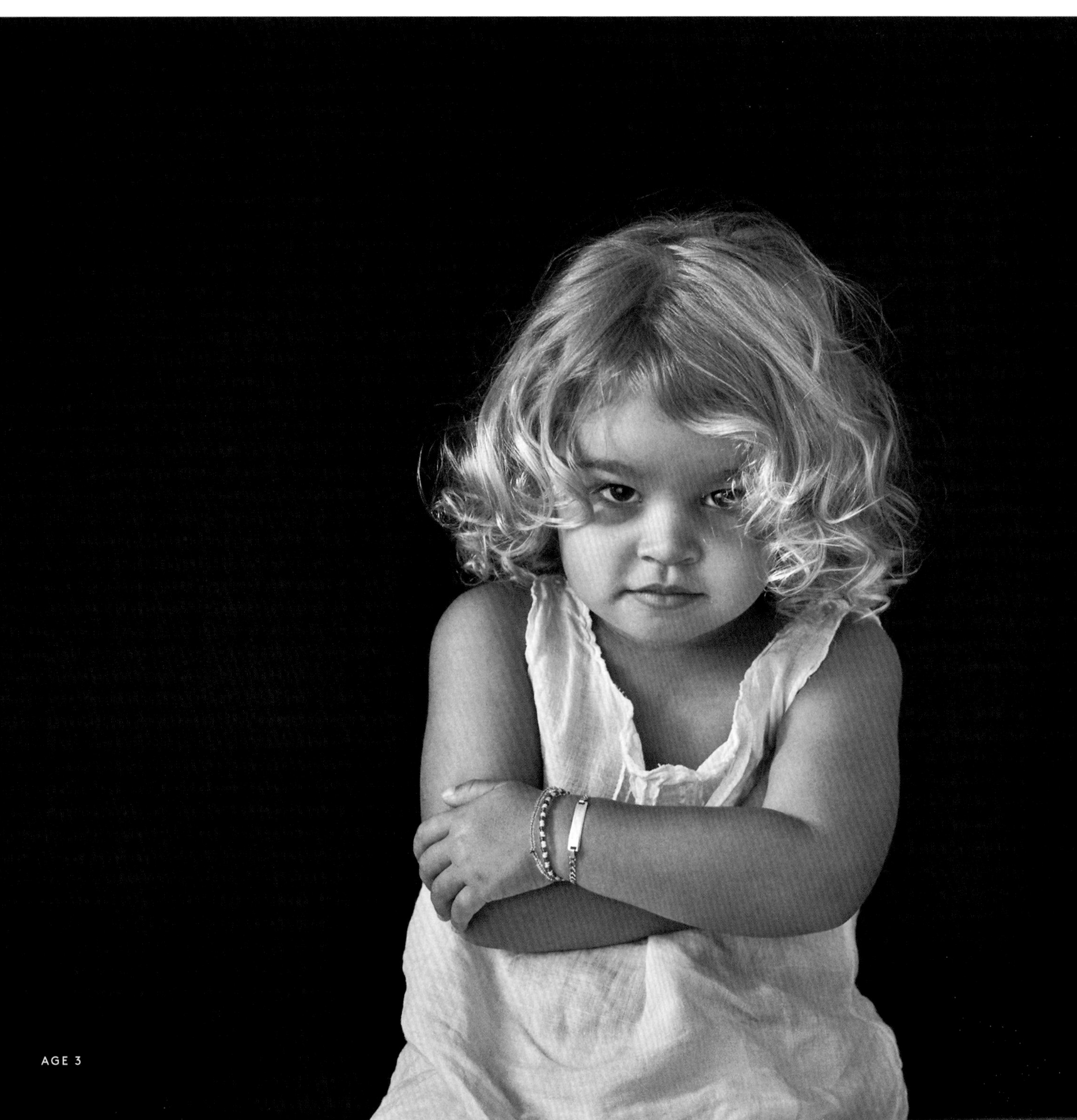
AGE 3

AVA

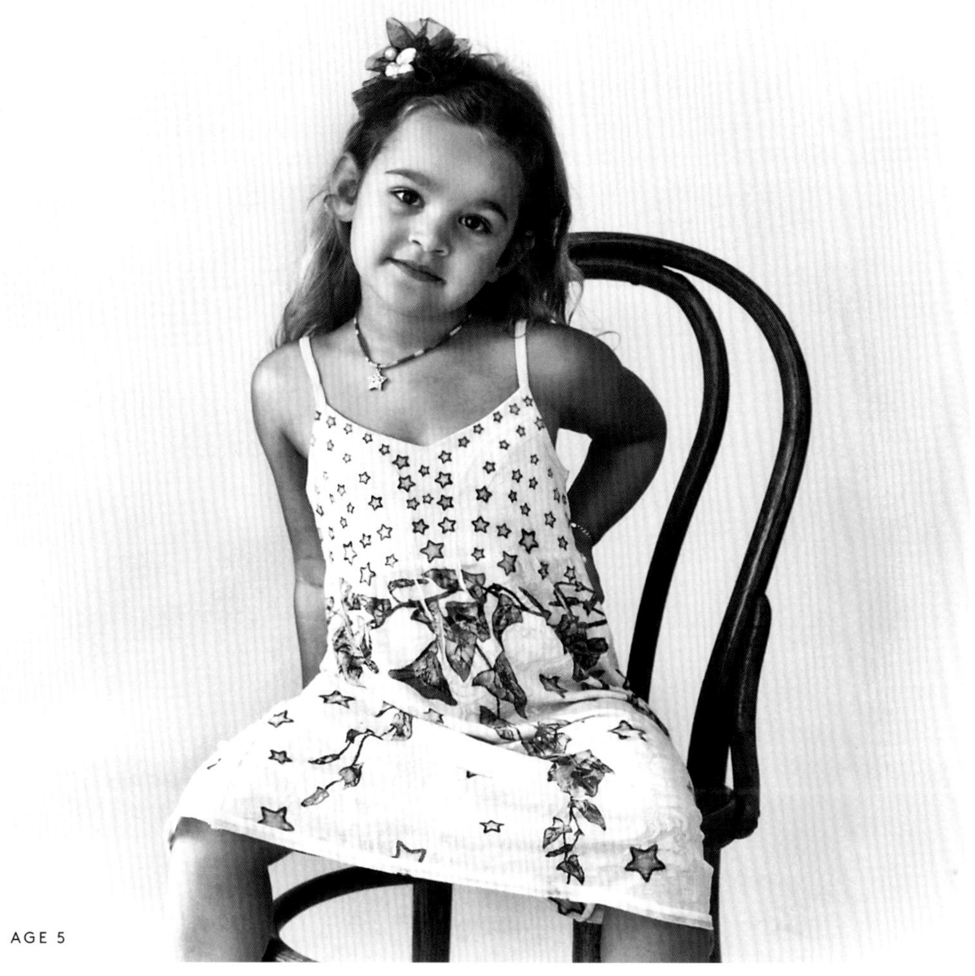

AGE 5

AVA, AT 6: Whenever my friends are sad, I hug them.

MEAGHAN, ERIKA & JENNY

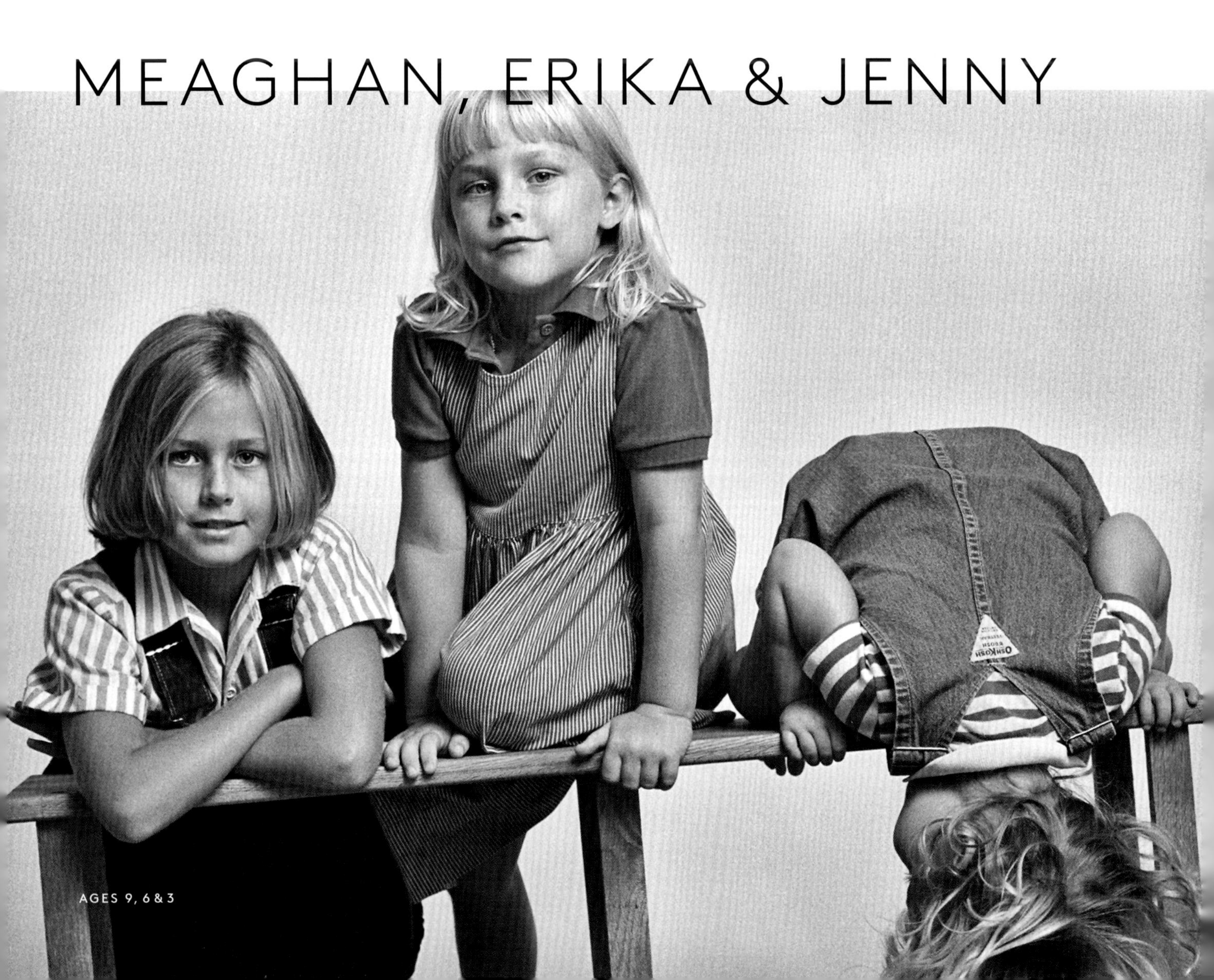

AGES 9, 6 & 3

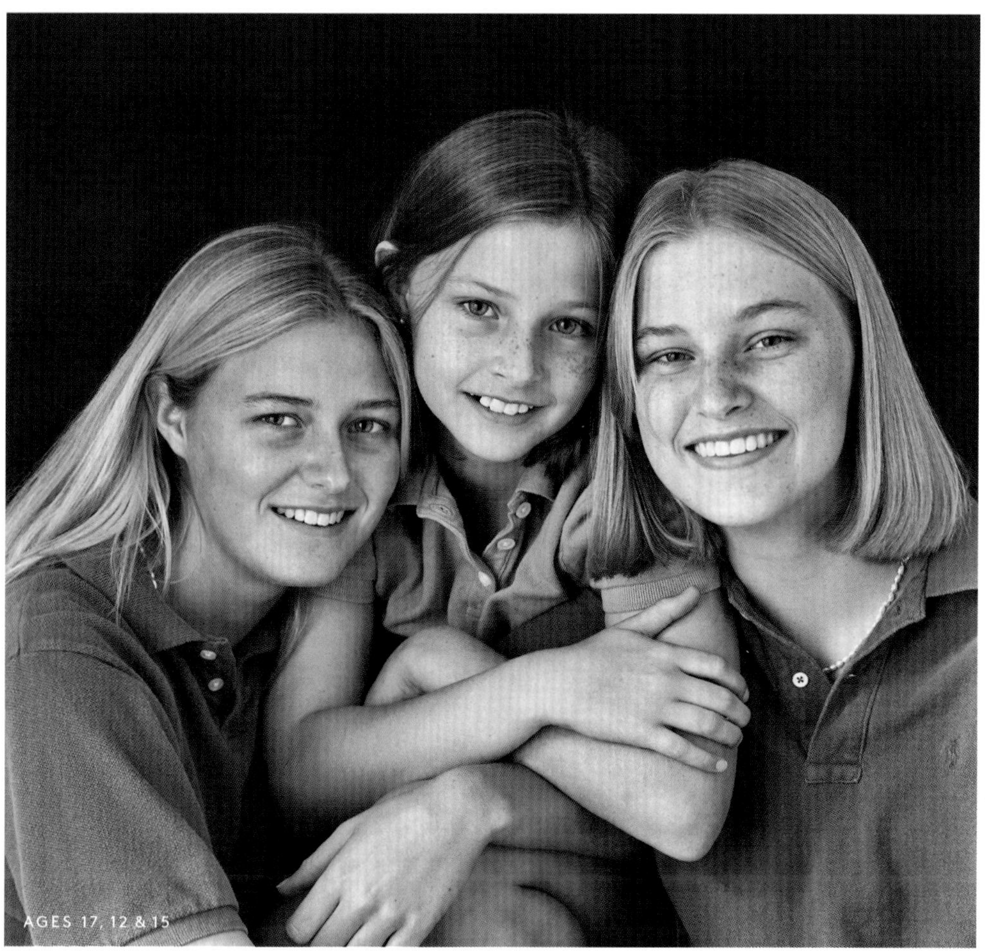

THEIR MOTHER: I feel happy when I walk by these pictures. Sometimes, "Oh I wish my kids were little again." No! In that moment it lasts forever — then the years whiz by. It's a wonderful time and also a grueling time. I was exhausted all the time. For basically healthy children, they weren't always healthy. One of my daughters broke so many bones — if they'd done a full body scan they would have arrested me. We all wish we could have held them longer. But the thing is to be present. One day I was in the house folding laundry. I had hired an au pair who was outside pushing one of the girls on a swing. I had an epiphany. I fired the nanny and hired a housekeeper. I wish I had done it earlier. When I look at these pictures, I'm nostalgic. Yet I'm happy for them to have grown up.

MARTIN & MICHAEL

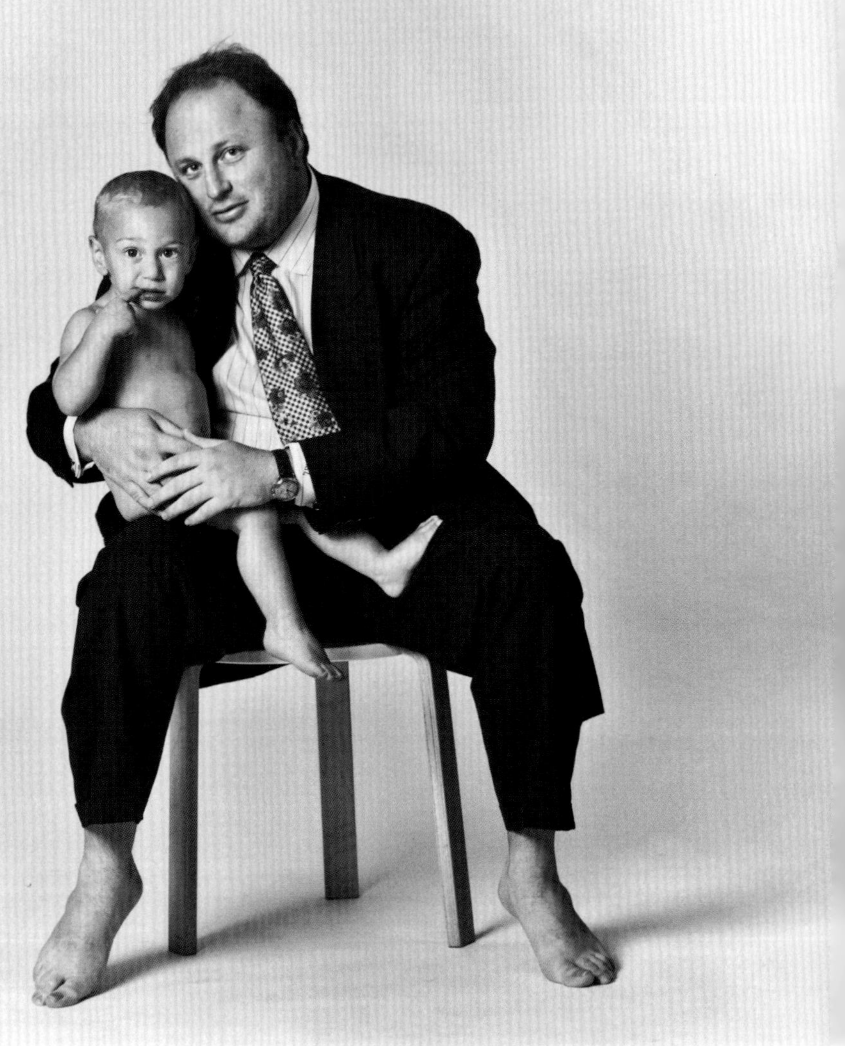

AGES 10mo. & 31

MICHAEL, AT 17: You can see that we're happy together, that it's a friendship, not just "How was school today?"

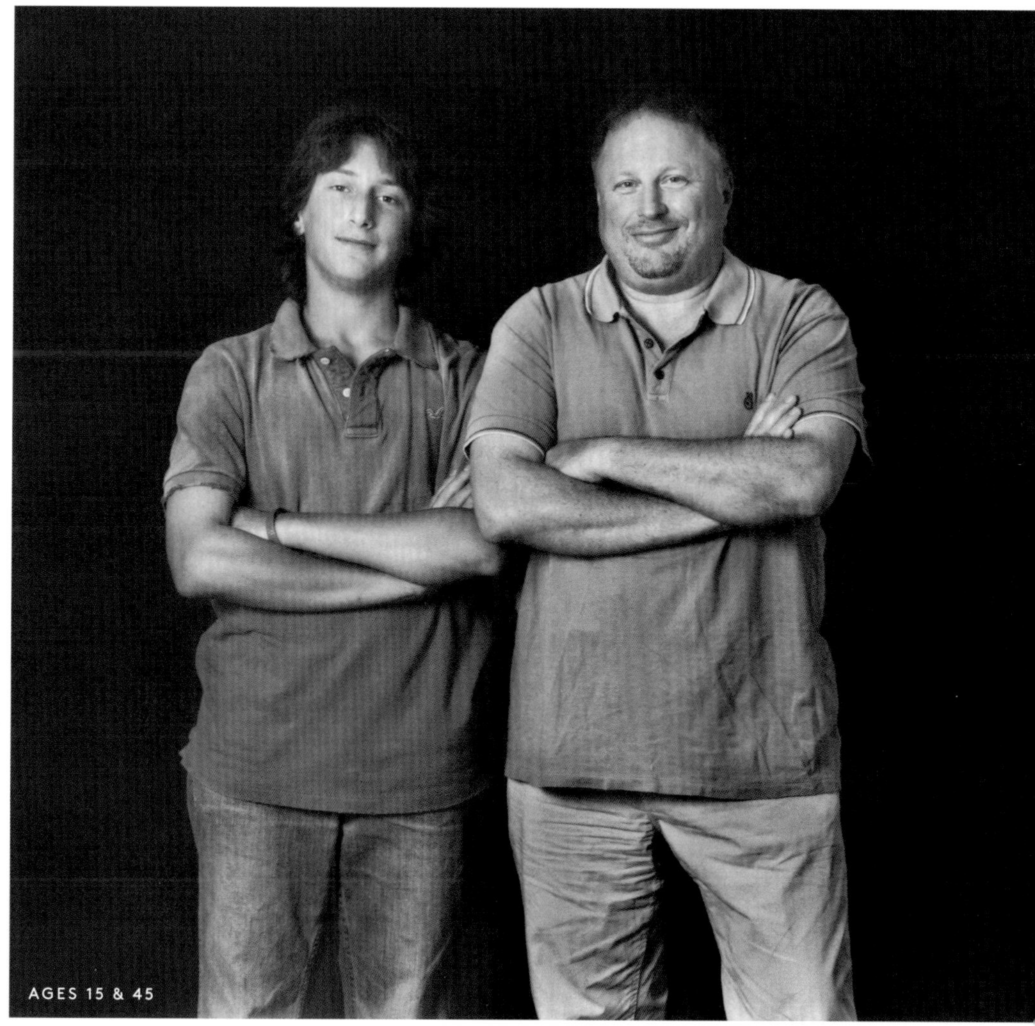

AGES 15 & 45

LILY, AT 15: I can remember in detail any significant event. I can recall what happened. I can remember my entire second birthday. RACHAEL, AT 20: I can't fake smile. LILY: She's very genuine. RACHAEL: I decided when Lily was very little that she'd be happier living in the apartment next door. LILY: I've always wanted to grow up faster than every one else. I'm still emotionally sensitive, especially toward animals and people with disabilities. I can walk into a place and see someone with a disability and it can make me cry. RACHAEL: I've always been overprotective, mothering. When people tell me not to mother then I say it's who I am. I have a tendency to worry. I don't understand how people expect me to change. I just want to be a mom. I have no interest in a job. But I like to help: I'm studying to be a social worker. LILY: I knew exactly that I was going to be a designer. I've always been good at giving advice. I've always wanted to own my own business. I didn't like childhood. I had disdain toward authority figures. I've thought that since kindergarten. Who are you to tell me what to do? I really know myself; I know exactly who I am. RACHAEL: Childhood was fast. I'm going to be twenty-one in June. I wish it would go back. LILY: We're such different people. I love having my picture taken. RACHAEL: I hate it.

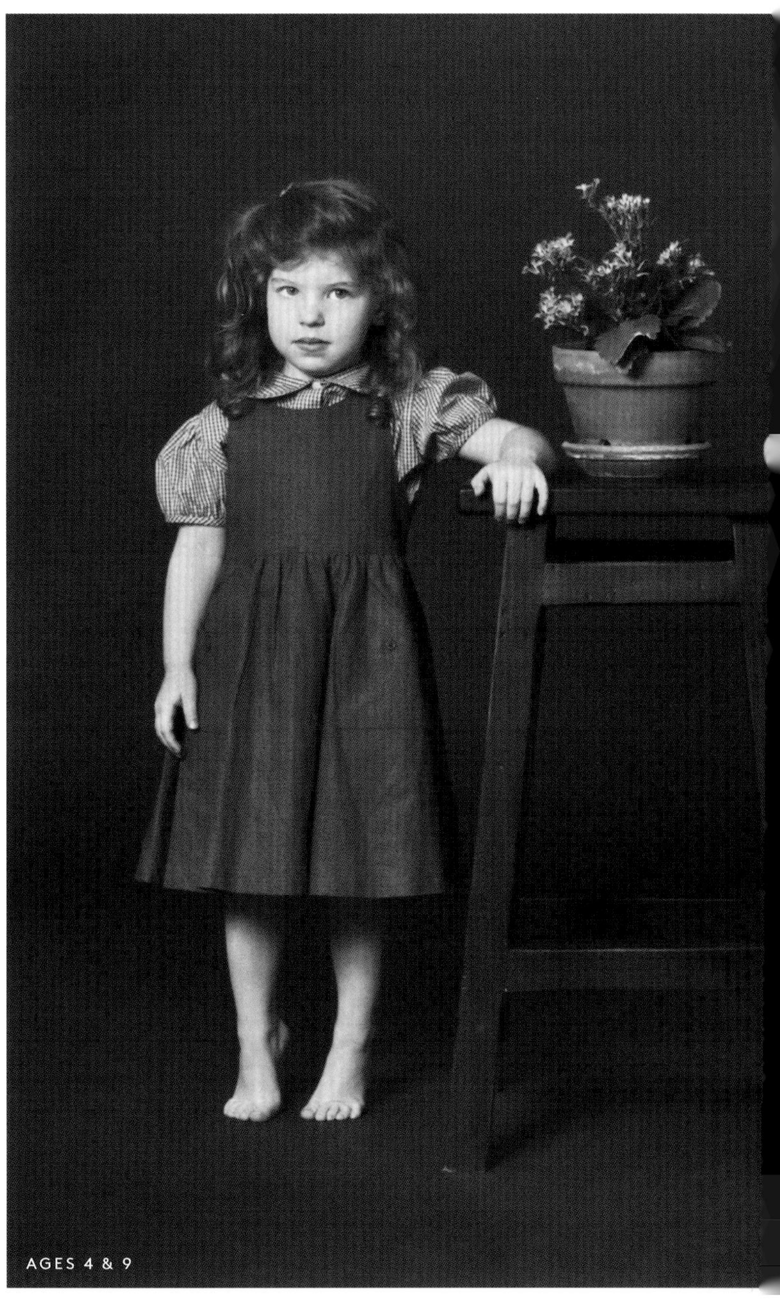
AGES 4 & 9

LILY & RACHAEL

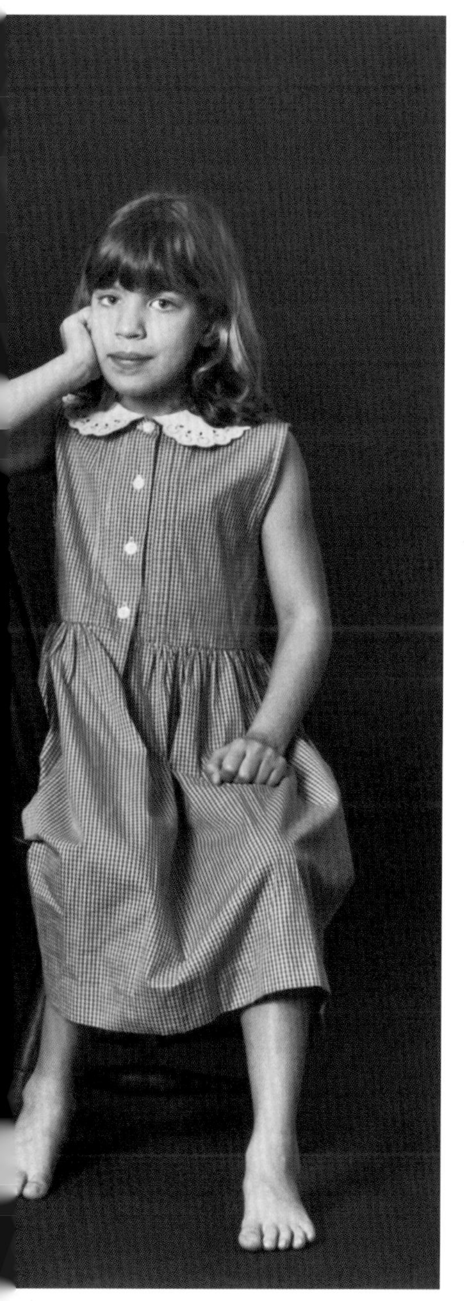

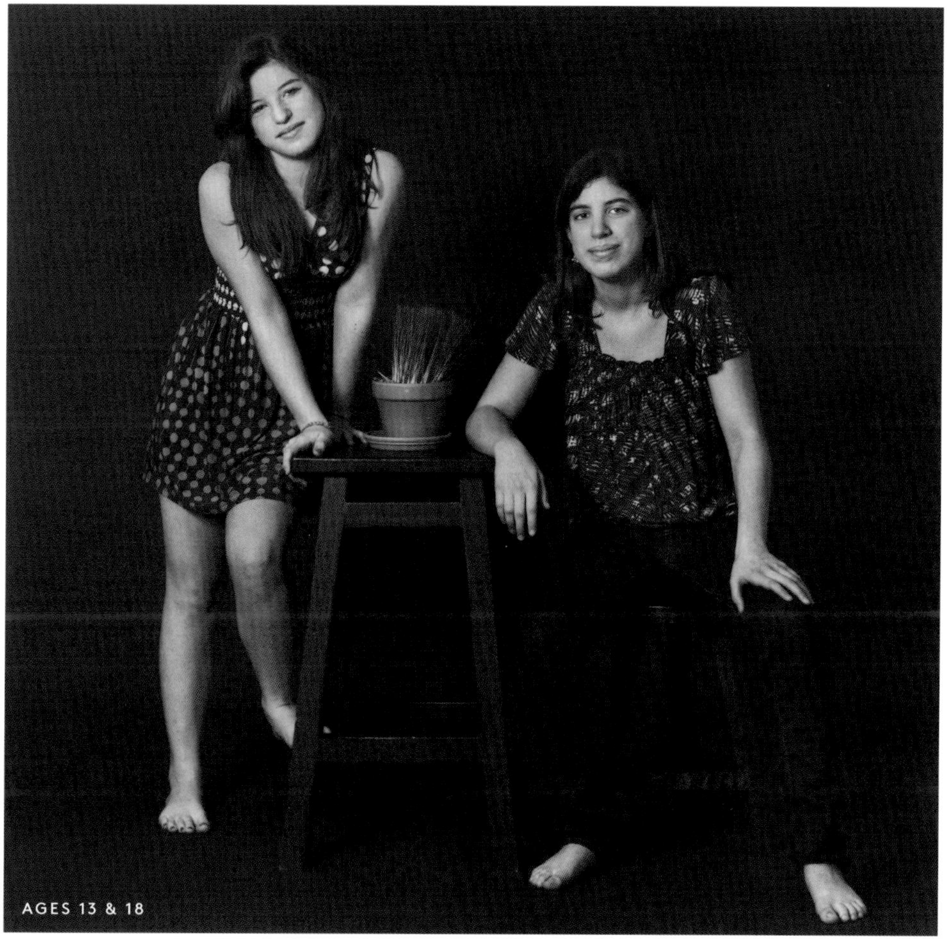

AGES 13 & 18

HIS MOTHER: This is who he was, loving and protective of me — "This is my mom, stay away." He's kind, sweet, protective — that's why everyone loved this picture. He was serious, not to be taken lightly. The next picture speaks less to me. He's an adolescent. We posed more. He's still sweet but also moving away — notice the angle of his head. He has a girlfriend.

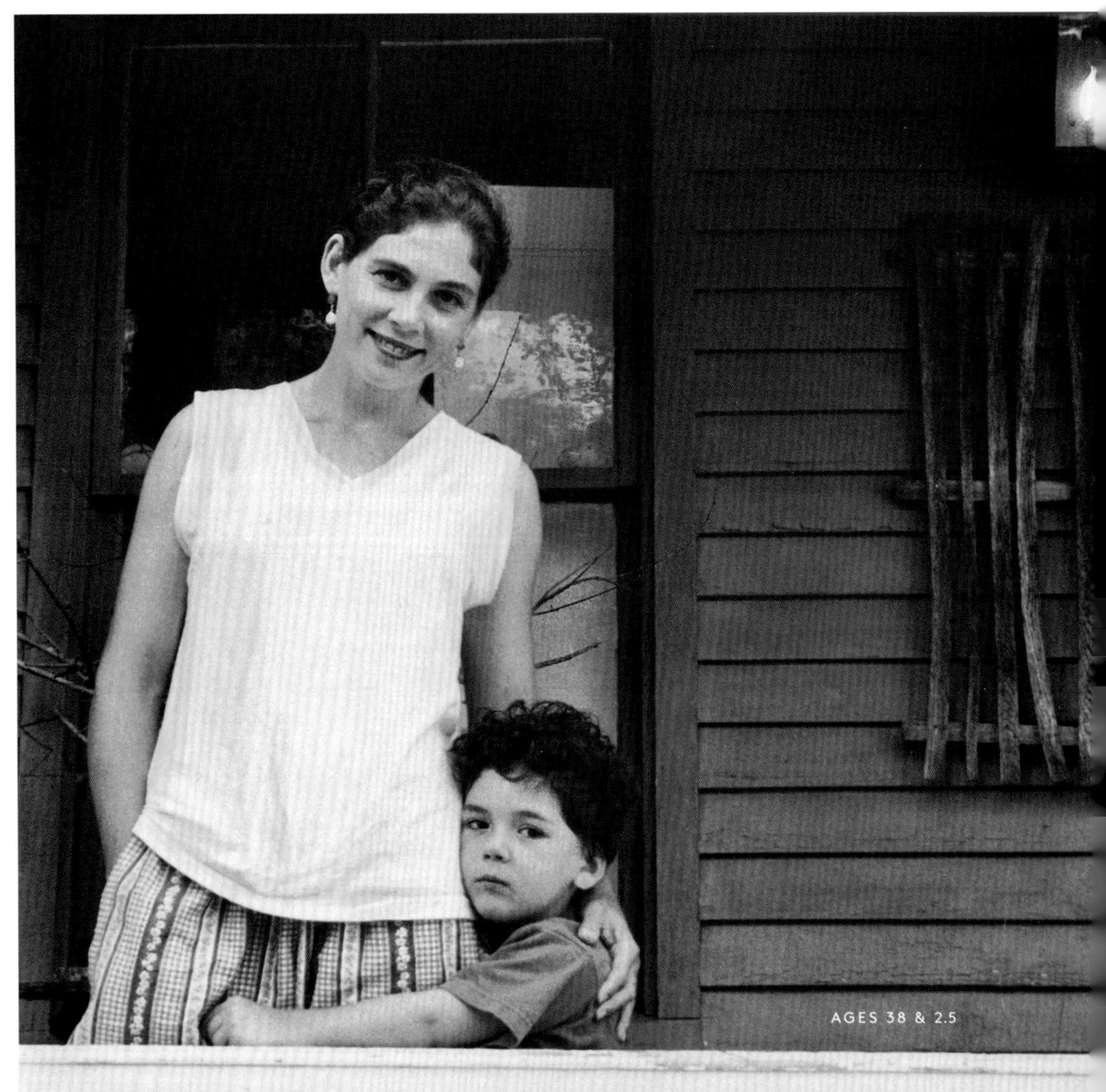

AGES 38 & 2.5

CATHY & ETHAN

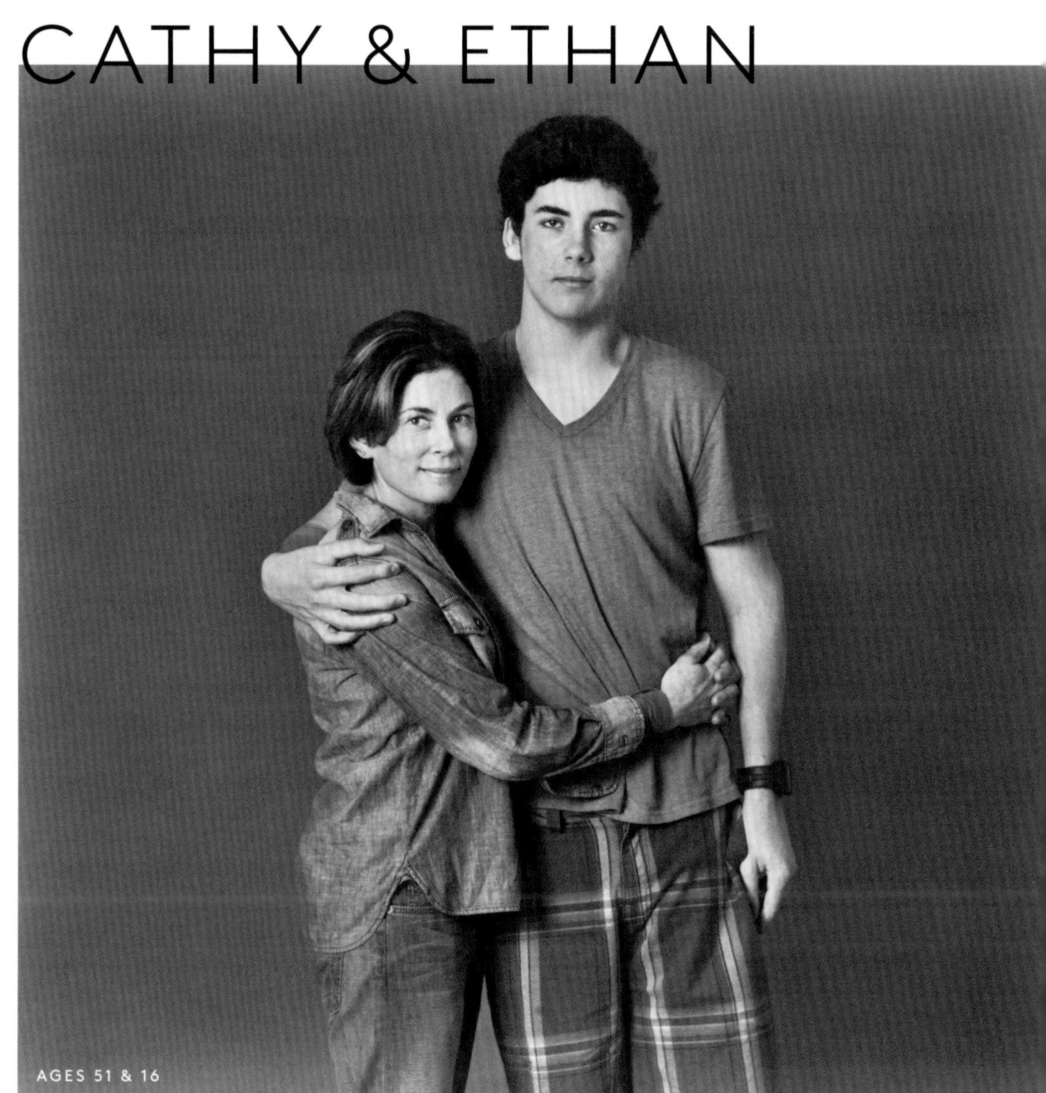

AGES 51 & 16

OLIVIA & JOHANNA

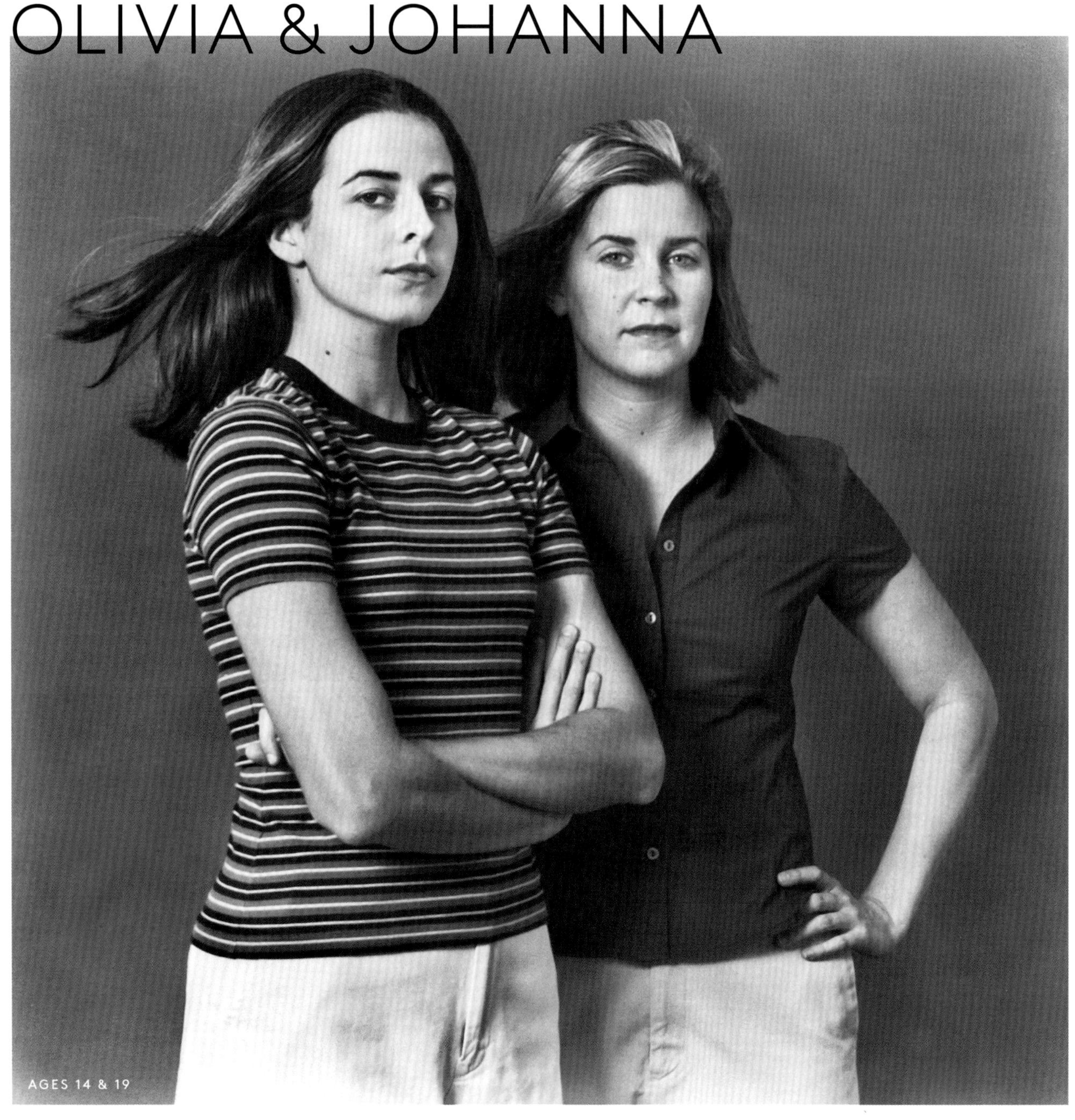

AGES 14 & 19

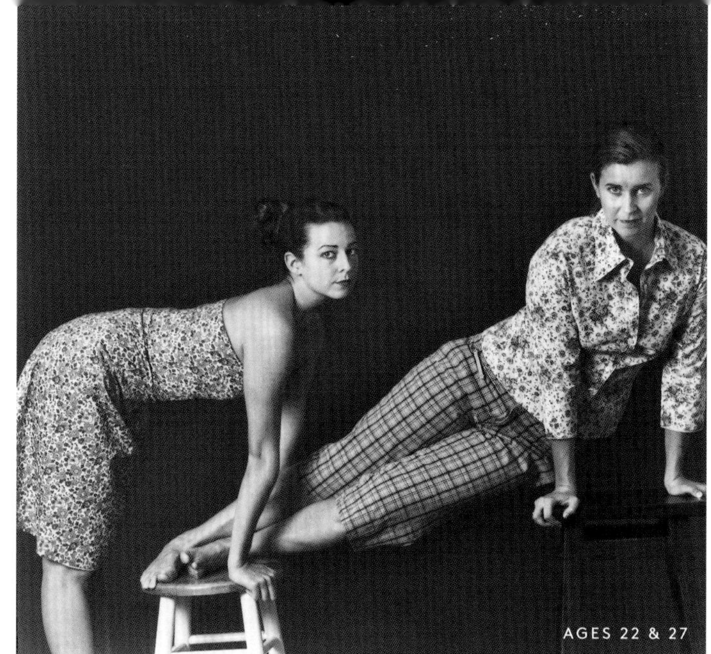

JOHANNA, AT 31: I loved riding bikes with my mother and sister. My mom towed Olivia behind her bicycle in this funny little buggy thing when she was too small for her own bike. We'd get grilled cheese or hamburgers and fries at the drug store. I'm nostalgic about that time. It sounds odd but I don't know that I ever had a clear picture of how my life would look. In some way I still don't. That can be scary but also liberating. I'm happy with where I am now. My sister and I both live in New York, although not together. She's a downtown girl and I moved to Brooklyn a year ago. We say we can't live together because she's allergic to my cat, Oscar, but really it's a better idea because we'd probably kill each other. I'd never be able to find any of my clothes, and she'd accuse me of stealing hers. I am often quite stubborn. I've been told I was that way as a toddler. I also tend to be very sensitive to others' feelings and want to help them resolve problems. I like being a fixer, sometimes to a fault.

ARI

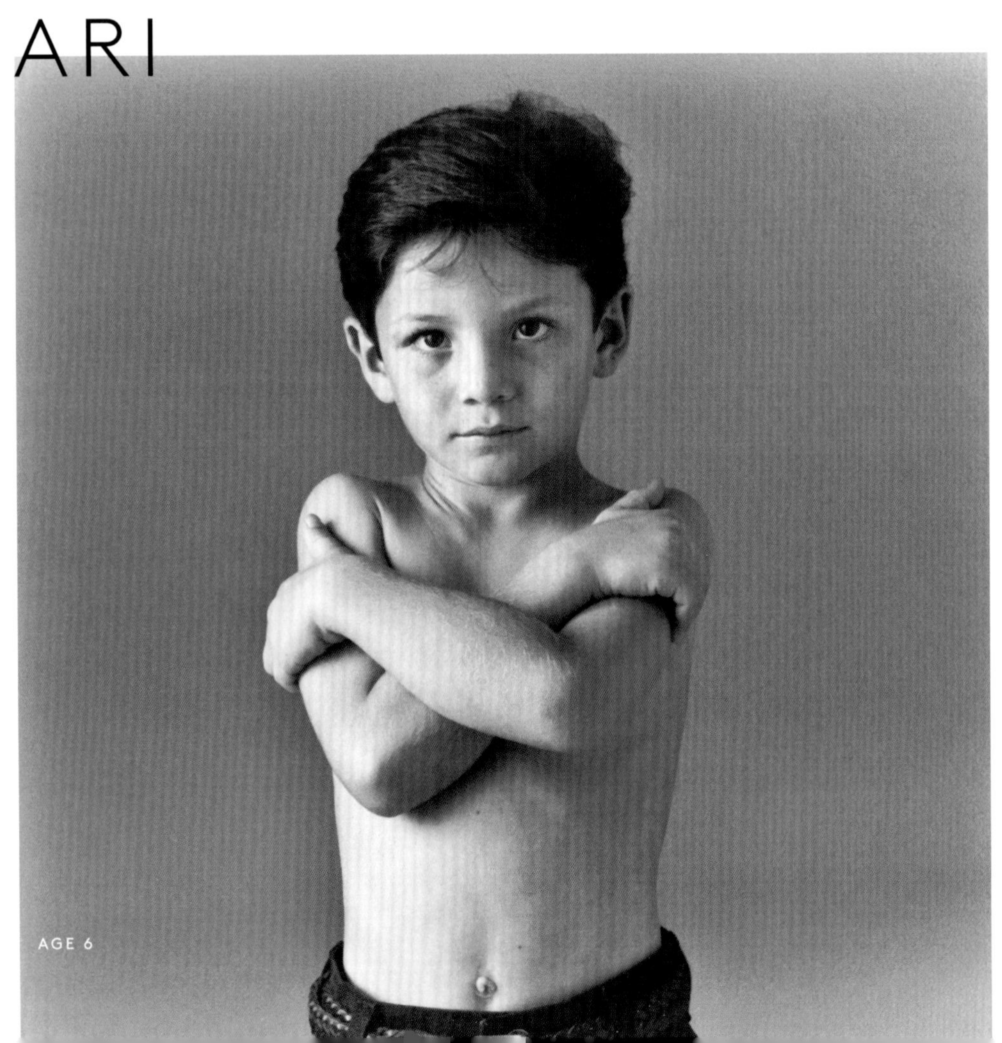

ARI, AT 23: When I was little, I loved when my dad took me by my ankles and hung me upside down. I loved sports. I loved to color. I loved my parents and did everything in the world to impress them. I called my mom "queen" because she meant (and still does) the world to me. The first picture shows how joyful I was. In the second picture, it seems like I am in deep thought, that I'm curious about the world. I love this picture. It describes a lot about my personality today. I am still a joyful person and definitely have a strong work ethic. I have not lived at home since I was in high school so I am used to being away from my parents. Even today and being so far away from my home I randomly get homesick.

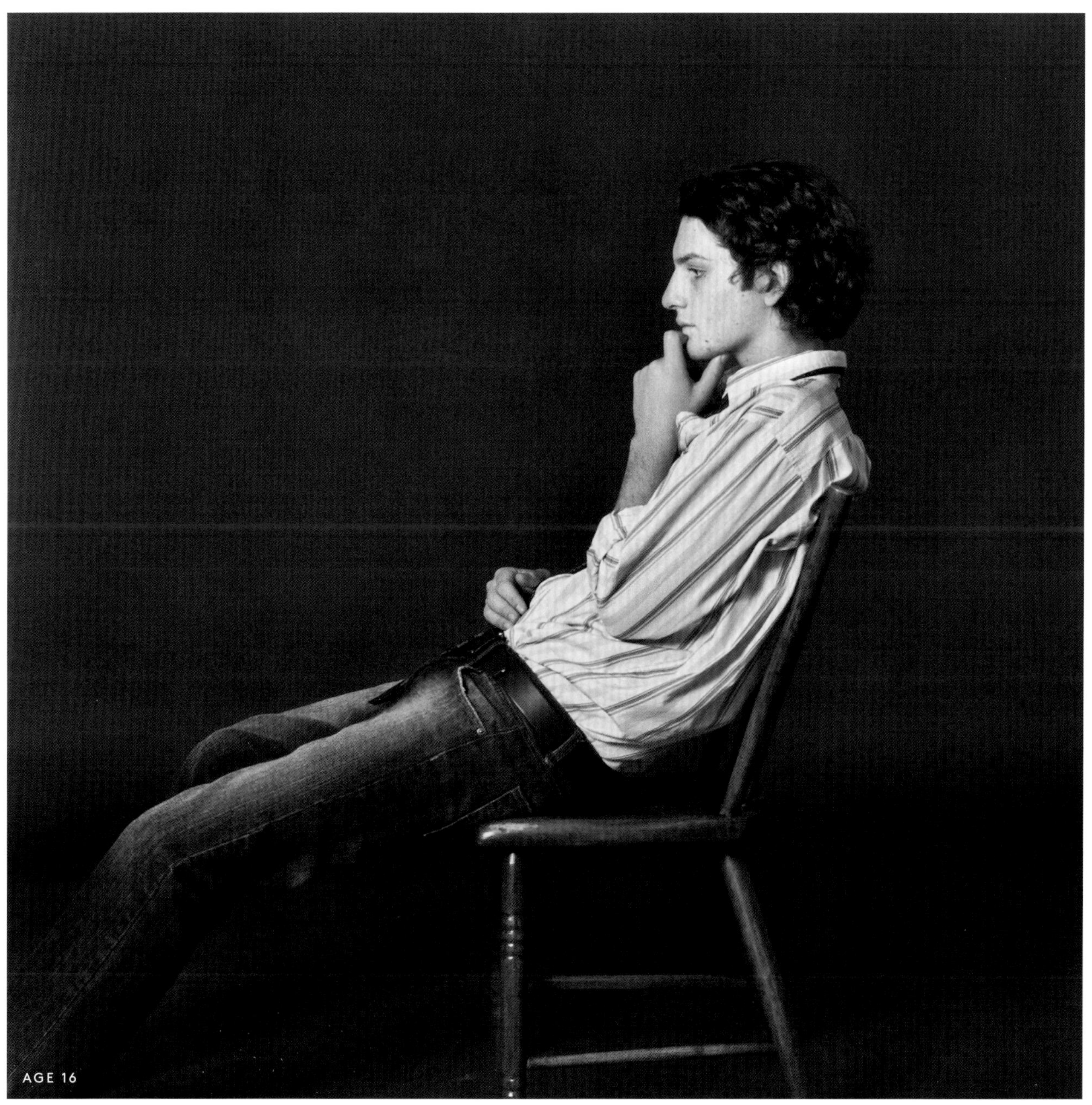

AGE 16

HANNAH & SOPHIE

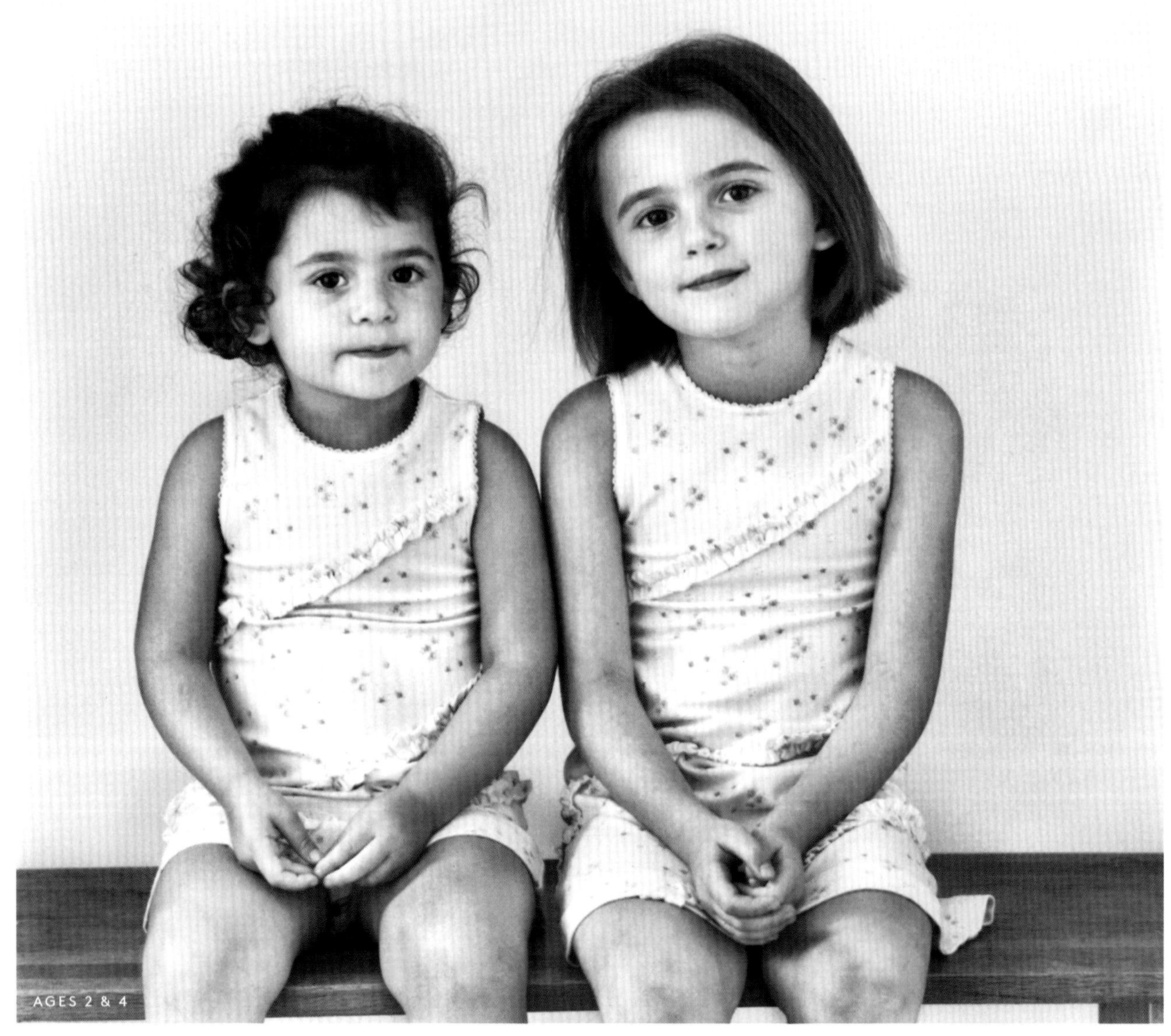

AGES 2 & 4

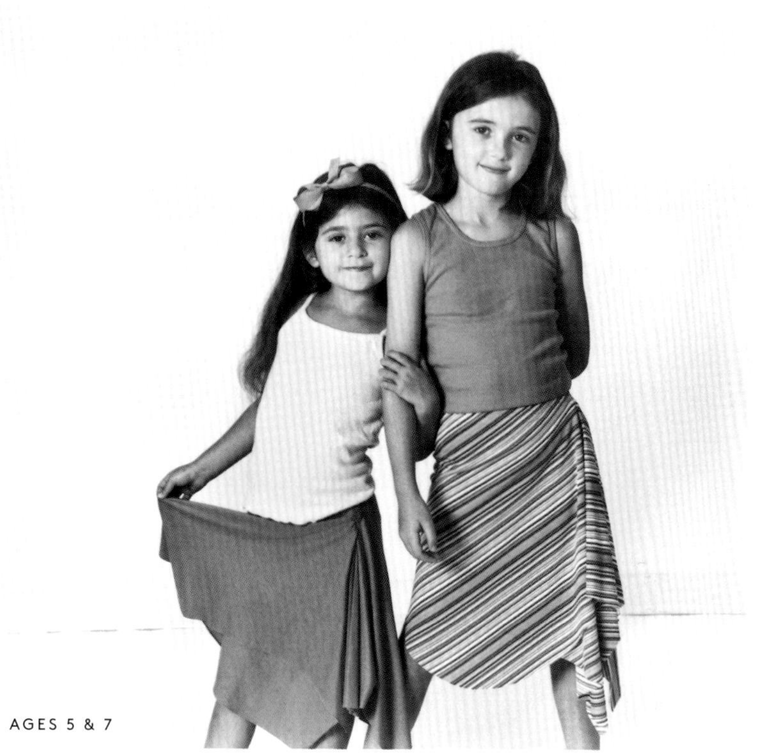

AGES 5 & 7

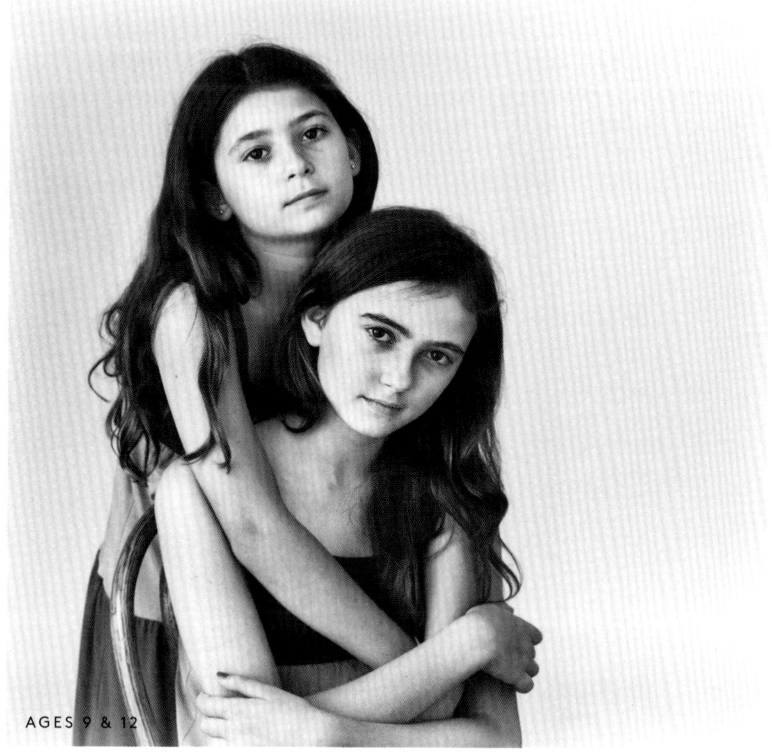

AGES 9 & 12

HANNAH, AT 5: I like being a little sister; I get to cry when she bothers me. One day I'll be a doctor or a teacher; my sister might be a builder or a hip-hop dancer. I'm going to have thirty kids because I love kids: I like them when they're little.

THE PHOTOGRAPHER: Years after I take the second photo of Coleman with his siblings, I receive his wedding announcement. I send him the photograph of himself in the army jacket.

COLEMAN WROTE ME BACK: "Thank you for the gift… I didn't have the ability to see it at the time but it is a fantastic picture. It arrived with my parents the morning after our son Homer was born and I looked at that picture of me and thought, for the first time, I remember him. Of course, but it was helpful to me to see where I was and how much heaviness I carried with me. I have grown into myself and can better carry that weight, whatever it is."

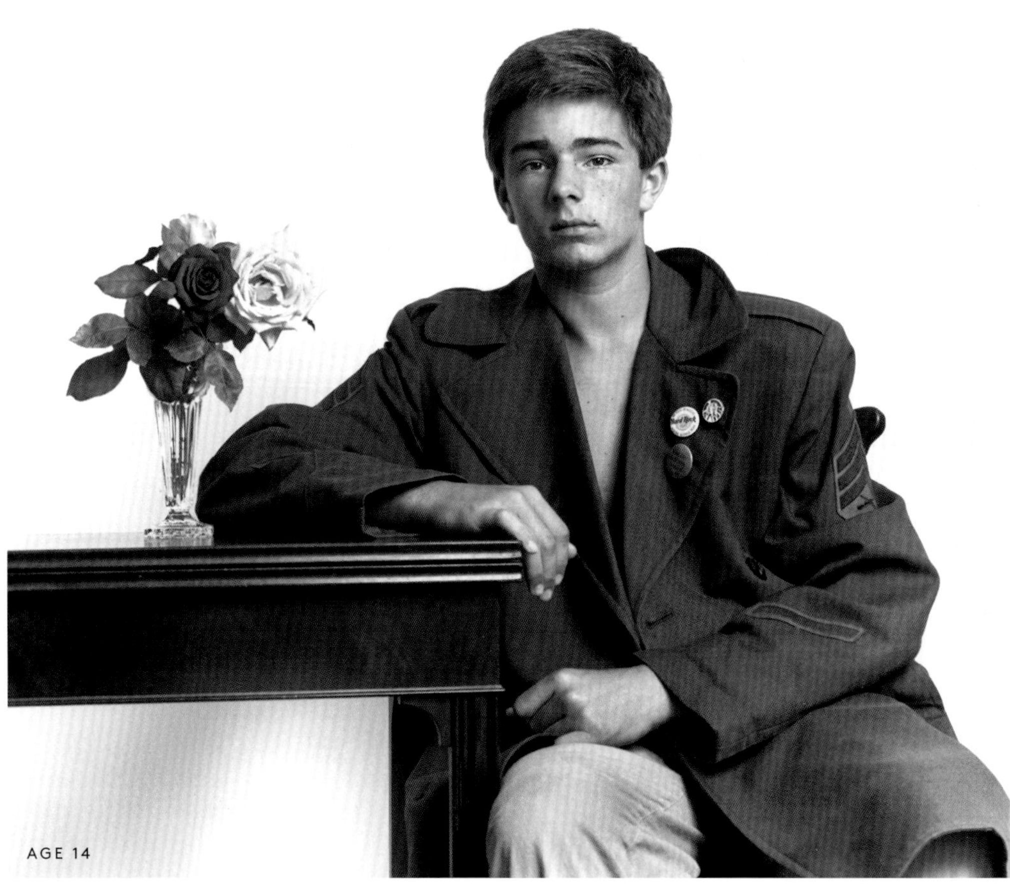
AGE 14

COLEMAN

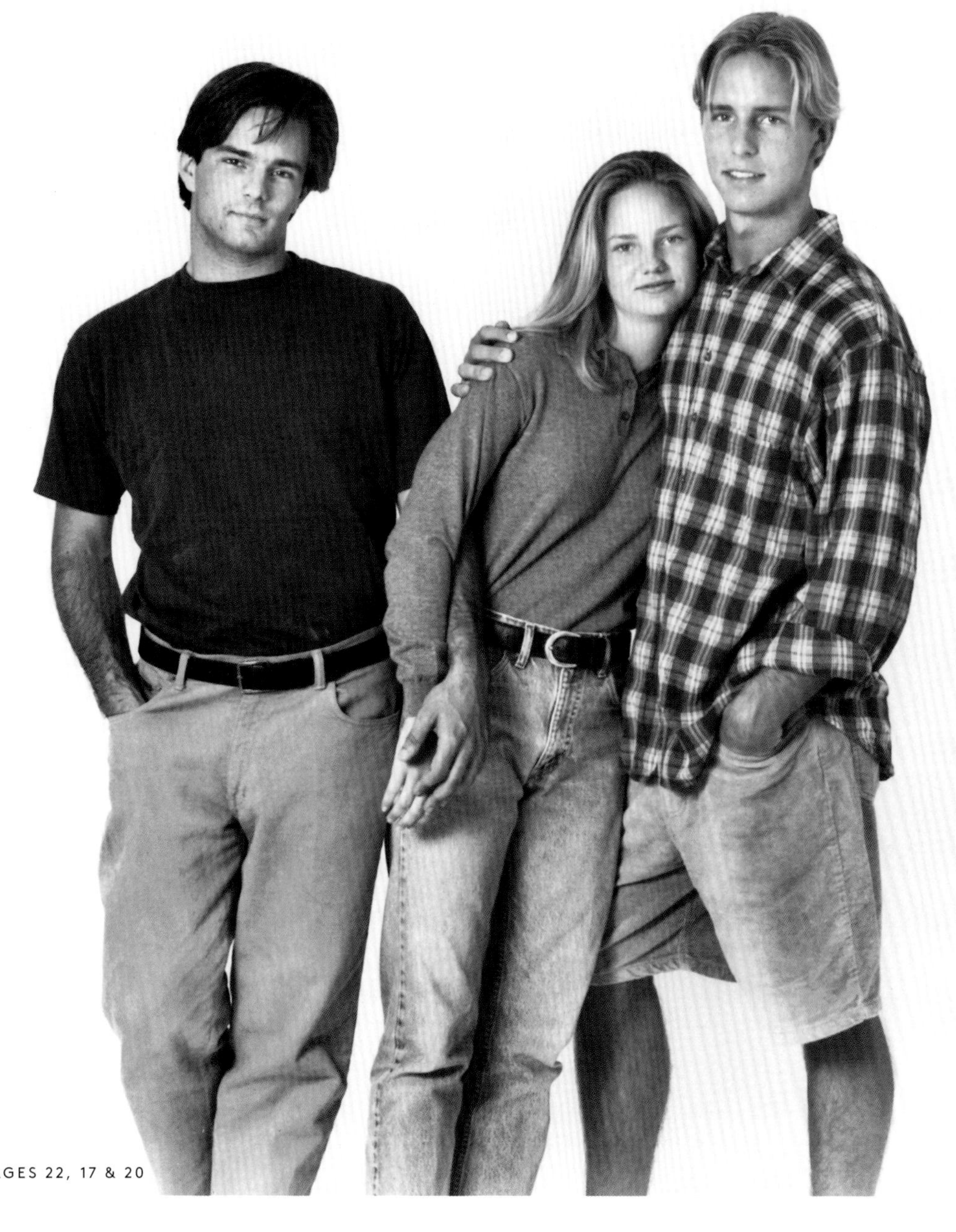

AGES 22, 17 & 20

AFTERWORD:

DAVE BARRY, PULITZER PRIZE WINNER

In the 1980s, when my son, Rob, was six or seven, I showed him all I knew about computer programming, which was this: Using a language called (I think) BASIC, I could instruct the computer to add two numbers and display the result.

This was a pathetically trivial feat of programming, kind of like using a bulldozer to break an egg. But Rob was thrilled. He was obsessed with numbers, math, measurements. He was always asking me how tall things were, how much things weighed, how fast things were going. If we were on a plane taxiing down a runway for takeoff, he would want to know at exactly what point we were going faster than a dog, then a horse, then a cheetah, and also what would happen if the cheetah jumped onto the wing... What then? Would we be safe? Could the cheetah break the window?

And of course, because a parent's job is to Know Things, I answered these questions. I told him how much the Chrysler Building, in my opinion, weighed. I told him how many atoms, in my opinion, were in a given glob of Play-Doh. I told him (this was the only answer I was sure of) that the cheetah could not break the airplane window. These answers satisfied Rob, in those days.

Soon after I showed Rob everything I knew about programming, he discovered that, in addition to adding, the computer could subtract, multiply, and divide. Soon after that he learned how to make it draw shapes on the screen. And soon after that he was creating elaborate programs — programs that had no apparent practical use, but that filled the screen with an impressive array of numbers and symbols and shapes and colors. I thought, wow, that's pretty cool, this little boy figuring out how to do that.

It was the first thing he did that I knew I could not do.

If you're a parent, you know where I'm going with this. Five minutes have passed, maybe six, and now Rob is a married man in his thirties. He's a reporter for a big newspaper; his specialty is computer database analysis. He sometimes tries to explain to me exactly what he does, but this is like a man trying to explain backgammon to a Labrador retriever. He never asks me questions about numbers anymore.

He does sometimes ask me about other things — weighty decisions of career and life — and I answer those as best I can. We both know I'm only giving him my best guesses, not verifiable truths like the cheetah on the wing. I wish I could be more certain for him, but he's a grown-up now, and he knows the world is an uncertain place.

Rob has a sister, Sophie, who's eleven. When she was three, I showed her how to draw a face — just a circle with crude squiggles for eyes, a nose, a mouth. She loved it, and started drawing faces of her own. It was instantly clear that she could draw far, far better than I could. Our house is now filled with her paintings and drawings. I sometimes wonder if she'll be an artist when she grows up. But it's still way too early to think about that. She's just a kid. Her world is school and homework and sleepovers and soccer and art lessons and Justin Bieber.

We have at least two more minutes.

ABOUT THE AUTHOR & PHOTOGRAPHER

Maggie Evans Silverstein is a portrait photographer living in Miami, Florida. Formerly an editor for *Tropic, The Miami Herald*'s Sunday magazine, she wrote features and essays that included her photographs, and a weekly column on art and architecture. Her photographs have appeared in national photographic magazines and been exhibited at local galleries.

ACKNOWLEDGMENTS

I want to give thanks to all the sitters in this book — each and every one has a place in my heart.

And to our inspirational children: Jennifer & Fred, Josh & Stef, Cathy & Steven, Joan & Dan, and Matthew.

And to the crew who gave me technical and philosophical and rise-and-shine support: Carol & David Kunstler, Maddy Blais, Marcie Ersoff, Norma Watkins, Margie Klein, Tammy Cohen, Steve Meeks, Ruth Greenfield, Nesie Summers, Dave Read, Bernice Steinbaum, Elinor Persky, Dave Barry, Jessica Jonap, and Mitchell Kaplan.

Published by Books & Books Press
Publishing Consultants: Ausbert de Arce & Mitchell Kaplan, Miami
Project and Creative Director: Petra Mason, Miami
Layout and design: Kaile Smith, New York City
Library of Congress Cataloging-in-Publication Date
Double Take by Maggie Evans Silverstein
ISBN: 978-0-9913271-0-2. Library of Congress Control Number: 2014938679

Printed in China.